Blackfoot Grammar

Thousands of people in Alberta and Montana speak Blackfoot, an Algonquian language. But the numbers are diminishing, and the survival of Blackfoot is in some danger. To help preserve the language while it is still in daily use, Donald G. Frantz and Norma Jean Russell collaborated on the *Blackfoot Dictionary*, published in 1989 to widespread acclaim, and revised in a second edition in 1995. *Blackfoot Grammar*, now available in paperback, is the companion volume to the dictionary, and provides a description and analysis of the major features of Blackfoot grammar and language structure.

It is intended to serve a variety of audiences, and the structure of the book reflects this. The first few chapters can be read by laypersons interested in the Blackfoot language. They also provide a basis for the more intensive and technical chapters which follow, intended for Algonquianists and advanced students of North American languages. A list of references and an index are included, along with an appendix on verb paradigms and one on phonological rules.

Based on decades of research, *Blackfoot Grammar* will be welcomed not only by those who wish to learn the language, but all those with an interest in native studies and North American linguistics.

DONALD G. FRANTZ is Professor of Native Studies, University of Lethbridge.

Blackfoot Grammar

Donald G. Frantz

UNIVERSITY OF TORONTO PRESS
Toronto – Buffalo – London

© University of Toronto Press 1991
  Toronto – Buffalo – London
  Printed in Canada

Reprinted in paperback 1997, 2000

ISBN 0-8020-5964-3 (cloth)
ISBN 0-8020-7978-4 (paper)

Printed on acid-free paper

Canadian Cataloguing in Publication Data

Frantz, Donald G.
  Blackfoot grammar

  Includes index.
  ISBN 0-8020-5964-3 (bound)
  ISBN 0-8020-7978-4 (pbk.)

  1. Siksika language - Grammar. I. Title.

  PM2342.F68 1991   497′.3   C91-093723-0

University of Toronto Press acknowledges the financial assistance to its publishing program of the Canada Council for the Arts and the Ontario Arts Council.

University of Toronto Press acknowledges the financial support for its publishing activities of the Government of Canada through the Book Publishing Industry Development Program (BPIDP).

Contents

Acknowledgements — vii

Preface — ix

CHAPTER ONE   The Blackfoot Alphabet — 1

CHAPTER TWO   Some Basics of Blackfoot Grammar — 7

CHAPTER THREE   Intransitive Verbs — 15

CHAPTER FOUR   More on Intransitive Verbs — 20

CHAPTER FIVE   Some Phonological Rules — 25

CHAPTER SIX   Tense and Aspect — 30

CHAPTER SEVEN   Four Verb Stem Types — 39

CHAPTER EIGHT   Transitive Inanimate Verbs — 43

CHAPTER NINE   Attached Pronouns — 47

CHAPTER TEN   Transitive Animate Part 1: Direct — 51

CHAPTER ELEVEN   Transitive Animate Part 2: Inverse — 55

CHAPTER TWELVE   Transitive Animate Part 3 — 59

CHAPTER THIRTEEN	Demonstratives	63
CHAPTER FOURTEEN	Possessives	69
CHAPTER FIFTEEN	Allomorphy	78
CHAPTER SIXTEEN	Complex Verb Stems, Part 1	84
CHAPTER SEVENTEEN	Complex Verb Stems, Part 2: Finals	99
CHAPTER EIGHTEEN	Some Concrete Finals	102
CHAPTER NINETEEN	Other Verb Paradigms	110
CHAPTER TWENTY	Nominalizations	116
CHAPTER TWENTY-ONE	Questions	132
CHAPTER TWENTY-TWO	Complement Clause Types	140
REFERENCES		145
APPENDIX A	Verb Paradigms	147
APPENDIX B	Phonological Rules	152
INDEX		157

Acknowledgements

Research upon which this work is based began nearly thirty years ago, so a very large number of people have had a part in it. I was fortunate that when I began to study Blackfoot (under the auspices of the Summer Institute of Linguistics), Allan Taylor, now of the University of Colorado but then a doctoral candidate at the University of California, Berkeley, had already spent a summer of research on the Blackfoot language in Montana. His generous sharing of his findings got me off to a comfortable start. Since that time he has contributed to my knowledge and understanding of Blackfoot structure in various ways, not the least of which is through his PhD dissertation (Taylor 1969).

Another person who has influenced my view of Blackfoot grammar over a period of many years and has brought various facts about the language to my attention is Gregory Thomson. More recently, Eung-Do Cook of the University of Calgary has made helpful suggestions and comments on the manuscript. I have also benefitted from suggestions of four anonymous reveiwers.

A large number of Blackfoot speakers have provided data and insights over the years. Those who gave extensive amounts are Irene Butterfly and Agnes Rider of the Blackfeet Tribe in Montana, and Rosie Ayoungman, Matthew Manyguns, Mike Peacemaker, and Frances and Bona Blackkettle of the Blackfoot Reserve in Alberta. More recently, Native students and faculty at the University of Lethbridge have provided data and corrected examples in earlier drafts of this work. Again, there were too many to mention them all, but Professor Leroy Little Bear, Martin Heavy Head, Mary Ruth McDougall, Lena Russell, Norma Russell, Sandra Bruised Head, and Mary Atoa come to mind. Mary's correction of several examples in the book are especially appreciated.

Finally, many non-Native students have helped improve this book as they have asked probing questions about its content. Among those who have contributed the most in this way are Marguerite Koole and Michelle Deering.

Preface

This work is intended to serve a variety of audiences.

Because of a desire for this work to be useful to laypersons interested in learning, or at least learning about, the Blackfoot language, the first few chapters are written in quite a different style from the later, more technical sounding chapters. But the later chapters build upon facts and concepts introduced in the early chapters, which, it is hoped, provide a relatively painless introduction to many of the necessary technical terms utilized in those later chapters.

Because linguistic concepts are utilized and all description is explicit, this work can also serve as a reference text for courses on the structure of Blackfoot, as well as a reference grammar for linguists and others interested in the structure of the language. Users should be warned, however, that a casual reading of early chapters will not prepare the reader for later chapters. Basic concepts must be understood as they are introduced, for later presentations depend upon them. The experience of students who have used drafts of this work has been that one needs to continually review previously introduced concepts, terms, and facts, because knowledge of these is assumed after they have been introduced. Frequent use of the Index is recommended in this regard.

Near the end of some sections, material will be found in a smaller font size and labeled 'Supplemental Material'. Such material is included for completeness' sake, but can be skipped without hindering understanding of later material.

The language here referred to as "Blackfoot" is that spoken on three Southern Alberta reserves: Blackfoot [Siksiká], centered about one hundred kilometers East-Southeast of Calgary; Blood [Kainaa], covering a large area between Cardston and Lethbridge; and Peigan [Aapátohsipi(i)kani], west of Fort MacLeod; as well as on the Blackfeet [Aamskáápipi(i)kani] reservation in Northwestern Montana. Blackfoot is a member of the Algonquian language family.

BLACKFOOT GRAMMAR

Donald G. Frantz

CHAPTER ONE

The Blackfoot Alphabet

The Blackfoot alphabet was designed to be read by native speakers of the language. Therefore, each letter represents a distinctive sound of the language, and predictable variations are not indicated because these are automatic for the native speaker of Blackfoot. For example, vowels are shorter before long (double) consonants than they are before single consonants, but because this vowel shortening is predictable (and automatic for native speakers) we still write the vowel as if it weren't shortened. Thus the first vowel of nínna 'my father' is shorter than the first vowel of nínaa 'man', though they are written the same because the presence of the double n in nínna is enough to predict the shortening.

While this is the ideal kind of writing system for native speakers of the language, it requires non-native speakers to learn consciously what is known subconsciously by those who learned the language as children.

This brief description will try to acquaint the reader with the approximate sound each letter represents, and give a few details of how sounds are affected by neighboring sounds.

The reader who wishes to learn to pronounce Blackfoot correctly, must, of course, hear and mimic the language as spoken by a native speaker.

THE VOWELS

There are three:

a has approximately the quality of a in English father, except before double consonants, where it has a quality more like the vowel of English cut.

sa	"no"	ánnia	"that's it / okay now"
ámo	"this"	máttso'kaawa	"he slept again"

i has a quality which varies from that of the i of English kiss to that of the i of machine; it always has the latter quality when long (written double - see below).

    ísska "pail"   miíni "berry"

o has a quality much like the o of English so, except before double consonants, in which case it has a quality more like the o of woman.

    óma "that one"   ónni   "his father"
    óki "hello / okay now"   sokóttaat "spit!"

VOWEL LENGTH (duration) is indicated by writing vowels double when long. It must be emphasized that by 'long vowels' we mean long in quantity (*not* quality, as the term 'long vowels' is used in English phonics). Thus oo represents approximately the same sound as does o in Blackfoot; the difference is in the amount of time they are sustained. Compare:

    áakokaawa   "he will rope"
    áakookaawa   "she will sponsor a Sundance"

DIPHTHONGS

ai varies among speakers and from dialect to dialect. Before double consonants (see below) it is about like the ai of English said:

    áínnisiwa   "he descends/falls"
    áíkkiwa   "he blows a whistle"

Before a glottal stop (written '; see below) or another vowel i it is about like the ai of English paid (though on the northern Blackfoot Reserve it may sound like the i of English bite.)

    áí'poyiwa   "he speaks"
    náíipisstsiwa "it's cloth"

In other positions of a word, this diphthong will sound like the ai of English plaid on the Blood Reserve, but like the ai of English paid on the Blackfoot Reserve.

    áípiima "he enters"   áípottaawa "airplane"

ao is like the aw of dawn (for those English speakers who pronounce the latter differently than they do Don); to approximate it, pronounce the a of English father with rounded lips.

    áókska'siwa "he's running"   áóttakiwa "bartender"
    ponokáómitaawa   "horse"

Before a glottal stop it may sound more like the <u>ou</u> of English <u>out</u>.

    ákao'toowa   "he has arrived"

oi is about like the <u>oi</u> of <u>coin</u>:

    nohkóíksi "my sons"   otahkóínattsi "yellow"

Before a long consonant, it may sound like the Blackfoot vowel **i** (see above) pronounced with rounded lips.

    nitáakotoissikópii   "I will go rest"

PITCH ACCENT, or prominence of a vowel or diphthong is indicated here by use of an acute accent over the vowel or diphthong; an alternative way to indicate Blackfoot pitch accent is by underlining accented vowels. The "prominence" mentioned in the preceding sentence consists primarily of a relatively higher pitch than that of contiguous syllables. Compare the following word pairs:

    ápssiwa "it's an arrow"   aohkííwa "it's water"
    apssíwa "it's a fig"   áóhkiwa "he's barking"

    ákaohkiimiwa "he's married"
    akáóhkiimiwa "he has many wives"

Because there is a gradual drop in pitch throughout an utterance, an accented syllable toward the end of a word of several syllables may actually be of lower pitch than an unaccented syllable earlier in the word; the accented syllable will still be relatively high in pitch as compared to the syllable which follows it, however, as in the following word:

    máátaissikópiiwa "he's not resting"

There are a few words in which the pitch falls noticeably during the pronunciation of a long vowel; in these cases only the first of the two letters which represent a long vowel is accented: <u>áaksoyiwa</u> 'he will eat'.[1] There are also sequences of a long vowel or diphthong (see below)

---

[1] There are also some cases in which the pitch falls through a sequence of three vowels; see chapter 15, section C.

followed by an accented vowel; these have a pitch which falls and then rises: maa<u>á</u>hsi 'her elder relation'; mao<u>ó</u>yi 'mouth'.

Pitch also falls during an accented vowel or diphthong which is immediately followed by a glottal stop (see below re. glottal stops).

    í'ksisakoyi "meat"   áí'poyiwa "he speaks"

SEMIVOWELS

w and **y** are glides with much the same quality as English <u>w</u> and <u>y</u> when the latter occur between vowels, as in a<u>w</u>are and <u>y</u>o-<u>y</u>o.

    á<u>w</u>aaniiwa "he says"   á<u>y</u>o'kaawa "he's sleeping"

(Note that **a+y** together sound like English e<u>ye</u>.)

CONSONANTS

m and **n** represent sounds virtually the same as the <u>m</u> and <u>n</u> of English:

    *m*a*m*ííwa "fish"   *n*í*n*aawa "man"

s is similar to the English sound usually represented by the same letter, except that the Blackfoot <u>s</u> is usually made with the tongue tip up, rather than behind the lower teeth as English <u>s</u> usually is. (The <u>s</u> of English pur<u>s</u>er is very much like the average Blackfoot <u>s</u>.)

    *s*a "no"   kii*s*tówa "you"   póó*s*iks "cats"

p, t, and **k** of Blackfoot are like their English counterparts except that they do not have the aspiration (puff of air) which usually follows <u>p</u>, <u>t</u>, and <u>k</u> in English; because of this nonaspiration, they often sound like <u>b</u>, <u>d</u>, and <u>g</u> to English speakers. English <u>p</u>, <u>t</u>, and <u>k</u> preceded by <u>s</u> in words such as <u>spin</u>, <u>sting</u>, and <u>skin</u> are about like the Blackfoot sounds.

    *p*oos "cat"   *t*akáa "who?"   *k*itsími "door"

h is a palatal fricative or "gutteral", much like the German sound written as <u>ch</u>. Like the German sound, it is greatly affected by the preceding vowel so that after <u>i</u> it is made at the highest point on the roof of the mouth, while after <u>o</u> or <u>a</u> it is made nearer the back of the roof of the mouth.[2]

---

[2] The letter **h** is also used for a sound like the <u>h</u> of English <u>hot</u> which occurs at the start of a few interjections. Since the palatal fricative occurs only following vowels, there is no danger of confusion as a result of using the same letter for a different sound in these interjections.

i*h*kitsíka "seven"   ó*h*kotoki "stone"   ksáá*h*koi "dirt"

' is an "interruption" made by momentarily closing the glottis (vocal chords) tightly, as English speakers do between the <u>oh</u>'s of the expression "oh-oh!" It is known as a **glottal stop**.

sa'áiwa "duck"   ní'sa "my older brother"
apí'siwa "coyote"   no'tsísi "my hand"

CONSONANT LENGTH (duration) is indicated by writing consonants double; this simply means that the articulation of such consonants is held a bit longer than it is for those consonants when written singly.[3] All consonants except <u>h</u> and <u>'</u> occur distinctively long:

kiip*í*p*p*o   "one hundred"   í*ss*ka   "pail"
áípo*tt*aawa   "he's flying"   iy*í*m*m*it   "laugh!"
nit*á*k*k*aawa "my friend"   ní*nn*a   "my father"
iks*í*s*s*iwa   "he is tough"   soká'p*ss*iwa   "he is good"

Phonetic Details And Some Spelling Conventions

Given the alphabetic system outlined above, there is a non-arbitrary spelling for almost every word of Blackfoot. However, in some cases, knowledge of the makeup of words can influence spelling of otherwise ambiguous sounds and sound sequences.

A relatively simple case is vowels at the end of a word. Since vowels in this position are generally voiceless, there can be no contrast between short and long vowels at the end of a word. However, we still write vowels as short or long in this position based on their length when a suffix is added. For example, one cannot tell by listening to the word <u>nitáópii</u> "I'm staying/sitting" that the final vowel is long. We write it as long because its length is observable in forms such as <u>aópiiyaawa</u> "they are staying/sitting" and <u>apiit</u> "sit!".

Vowel length is difficult, if not impossible, to discern before a glottal stop. However, if knowledge of the makeup of the word leads one to expect a long vowel in this position, we write it as such. For example, when the 'associated instrument or tool' suffix <u>-a'tsis</u> is added to a stem ending in <u>a</u> or <u>aa</u>, we spell the resulting sequence with a long **aa**. So <u>isttókimaa'tsis</u> 'drum' is so spelled because we know the verb stem <u>isttokimaa</u> 'drum' from which it is formed

---

[3]Most English speakers get a similar effect across word boundaries in English phrases such as <u>sick cow</u>, in which the phonetic [k] at the end of <u>sick</u> combines with the initial phonetic [k] of <u>cow</u> to give a long phonetic [k:]; this is quite like the <u>kk</u> of Blackfoot (except that Blackfoot <u>kk</u> lacks the aspiration of English <u>k</u> - see above.)

ends in the vowel **a**.

A non-arbitrary decision regarding vowel length before **h** can be made based on a regular phonetic rule of Blackfoot. If a vowel is voiced before **h**, it is interpreted as a long vowel, because only long vowels remain voiced in this position. So we write nitsíípiihpinnaan 'we sat/stayed' with a long **ii** because the vowel remains voiced before the **h**, even though the [i] sound before the **h** is not noticeably long. To this we can compare nitsíípihpinnaan 'we have archery equipment', in which the **ih** is a completely voiceless syllable (see pronunciation notes at the end of chapter 3).

It was stated near the beginning of this chapter that vowels and diphthongs have a slightly different quality when they are immediately followed by long consonants. In such a position, **a**, **i**, and **o** sound like the vowels of English cut, kiss, and bush, respectively. Though not stated earlier, this effect on vowel and diphthong quality before long consonants is present even if an s separates the vowel and long consonant. So, for example, the ai of áísttsiiwa 'it hurts' sounds like the ai of English said even though the diphthong is not immediately before the tt. However, the situation is even more complicated than this: *long* **aa**, **ii**, and **oo** retain their usual qualities even before long consonants, though in such a position their duration is reduced. So, for example, if one hears a vowel like the a of father and it is followed by a long consonant, then that sound should be spelled aa.

Supplemental Material

A more complex case is the phonetic sequence [o^i'ss], which can represent not only **oi'ss**, but **o'yss** and **oyss** as well. It can represent **o'yss** because anticipation of the **y** tongue position during the glottal stop produces a phonetic diphthong. It can represent **oyss** because a predictable glottal stop is heard whenever a glide (**w** or **y**) or nasal (**m** or **n**) is immediately followed by s. In cases such as this, one must either make an arbitrary choice or be guided by grammatical analysis of the word involved, if the grammatical makeup of the word is known. In this particular case, if the sequence [o^i'ss] is part of the sequence [oo^i'ssini] 'eating', it is analyzable as **ooyi**, the *vai* stem 'eat', plus the suffix **hsin**, which makes nouns from intransitive verbs. Given the fact that **ihs** is generally realized as **ss**, we spell the word as **ooyssini**. We do not need to include the predictable glottal stop, though to do so would not in any sense produce an incorrect spelling.

CHAPTER TWO

Some Basics of Blackfoot Grammar

In the discussion of nouns and verbs to follow in this and the next chapter, it will be necessary to distinguish between **words** and **stems**. By definition, a word is pronounceable by itself, whereas a stem is the core of a word and generally needs a prefix or suffix added to make it a word. For example, we shall see below that the Blackfoot **noun stem** meaning "man" is <u>ninaa</u>, but this cannot be used as a word unless a suffix is added; the suffix <u>wa</u> can be added forming the singular noun <u>nínaawa</u> 'man', or the suffix <u>iksi</u> can be added forming the plural noun <u>nínaiksi</u> 'men'. (Notice that this differs from the situation in English, where the stem <u>man</u> alone can be used as a word.)

A. GRAMMATICAL GENDER

In popular usage, the term 'gender' is associated almost exclusively with sex categories. This usage corresponds to the fact that English nouns are classified as masculine, feminine, or neuter, and this classification is reflected in the choice of singular pronouns <u>he</u>, <u>she</u>, or <u>it</u>. But technically, the term 'gender' can be applied to any at least partially arbitrary classification of nouns in the grammatical system of a language. To make it clear that we are using the term in the technical sense, we will refer to such noun classification as **grammatical gender**.

Blackfoot, like other Algonquian languages (such as Cree, Chippewa, Micmac, etc.), classifies noun stems into two groups which are often labeled **animate** and **inanimate**. (In the Blackfoot Dictionary of Stems, Roots, and Affixes [henceforth, "the Dictionary"],[4] animate gender noun stems are labeled *nan* and inanimate gender noun stems are labeled *nin*.) All Blackfoot noun stems belong to one of these two grammatical gender classes, and this classification is evident throughout Blackfoot grammar. For example, we shall

---

[4]Frantz and Russell (1989).

see below that there are two ways of pluralizing a noun, depending upon the grammatical gender of that noun.

It is important to realize that grammatical gender classification says very little about how people view the world. (*E.g.*, in French the noun la table 'table' belongs to the so-called feminine gender class, but surely the native speaker of French doesn't think there is anything feminine about a table.) So the fact that Blackfoot noun stems such as pokón 'ball', íssk 'pail', and isttoán 'knife' are classed with noun stems such as aakíí 'woman', pookáá 'child', and imitáá 'dog' as being of animate gender should not be construed as an indication that the Blackfoot speaker thinks of balls, pails, and knives as somehow "alive". **Grammatical gender is a classification of the noun stems themselves, not of the entities to which they refer.** Nevertheless, the English speaker learning Blackfoot can be sure the words for animals, people, or spirits will be of animate gender. But the gender of other nouns simply must be memorized (though there are some other natural groupings which are helpful to recognize; *e.g.* stems for most metal tools are of animate gender). Here are a few more noun stems which are unpredictably animate in gender:

moápssp	"eye"	po'táá'tsis	"stove"
naató'si	"sun"	atapíím	"doll"
ksisíís	"thorn"	mookítsis	"finger"

B. NOUN NUMBER

Noun stems take suffixes which mark them as singular or plural. A singular animate gender noun has -wa,[5] and plural animate gender nouns have -iksi:

ponoká*wa*	"elk"	ponoká*iksi*	"elk (pl.)"
natáyo*wa*	"lynx"	natáyo*iksi*	"lynx (pl.)"

w is always dropped after a consonant, so the animate singular suffix appears to be -a after stems which end in a consonant; consequently the singular of 'cat', *e.g.*, is poosa, not *pooswa:

póós*a*	"cat"	póós*iksi*	"cats"
íssk*a*	"pail"	íssk*iksi*	"pails"

Inanimate gender noun stems take -yi, in the singular and -istsi in the plural:

i'ksisako*yi*	"meat"	i'ksisako*istsi*	"meats"
ómahksíkimi*yi*	"lake"	ómahksíkimi*istsi*	"lakes"

---

[5]Certain speakers omit the suffix -wa under as yet undetermined conditions. And many young speakers seem never to use it.

Like w̱, y̱ is always dropped after a consonant, so the inanimate singular suffix appears to be -i̱ after stems which end in a consonant:

níípi	"leaf"	níípistsi	"leaves"
mo'tokááni	"head"	mo'tokáánistsi	"heads"

Long vowels are shortened before any suffix that starts with a vowel, such as the pluralizers. Compare the following singulars and plurals; note that the long vowel at the end of the stems (*e.g.* nínaa) is short in the plural:

nínaawa	"man"	nínaiksi	"men"
kakkóówa	"pigeon"	kakkóíksi	"pigeons"
mamíiwa	"fish"	mamííksi	"fish (pl.)"
aohkííyi	"water"	aohkíístsi	"waters"

There is a large number of noun stems which have an ṉ or s̱ that is present only before certain suffixes; a few stems have an m̱ which is present only before the same suffixes. When listing such stems we will indicate these **non-permanent consonants** by the symbols M̱, Ṉ, and S̱, respectively.[6] M̱, Ṉ, and S̱ are lost (*i.e.* do not show up as m̱, ṉ, and s̱) before the pluralizers:

Stem	Gloss	Singular	Plural
áto'ahsiM	"sock"	áto'ahsima	áto'ahsiiksi
máíipssiM	"belt"	máíipssimi	máíipssiistsi
asóka'siM	"dress"	asóka'simi	asóka'siistsi
pokóN	"ball"	pokóna	pokóíksi
isttoáN	"knife"	isttoána	isttoáíksi
áwanááN	"rattle"	áwanáána	áwaanáíksi
atsikíN	"shoe"	atsikíni	atsikíístsi
moksíS	"awl"	moksísa	moksííksi
ksisííS	"thorn"	ksisíísa	ksisííksi
mo'tsíS	"hand"	mo'tsísi	mo'tsíístsi
niitóyiS	"tipi"	niitóyisi	niitóyiistsi

---

[6]This device is not used in the Dictionary. There, stems are listed with such non-permanent consonants present; one can determine that they are non-permanent by comparing the examples which are provided.

C. PARTICULAR vs. NON-REFERRING

Sometimes when using a noun, we don't have in mind a particular item (or group of items) from the class of things that we name by that noun; just any one (or bunch) will do. For example, you might send a son or daughter to the store with the following instructions: "Get a loaf of bread, some milk, and a dozen apples." You don't have any particular loaf of bread, carton(s) of milk, or dozen apples in mind, so the nouns <u>bread</u>, <u>milk</u>, and <u>apples</u> **do not refer** to any particular items. Or you may use a noun in such a way that it **cannot refer** to an actual entity. This would be true in sentences such as "I don't have any milk." or "I wish you had some apples." In either case we say that the words <u>bread</u>, <u>milk</u>, and <u>apples</u> are **non-referring**.

At other times we may wish to refer to a particular item or group of items, as in these sentences:

'Give me that loaf of bread.'
'Your milk is turning sour.'
'I bought a dozen apples and my family ate them in one day.'

Here because the speaker has a particular loaf of bread, some particular portion of milk, and a particular dozen apples in mind, we say that these nouns are **particular** in reference. The endings on Blackfoot nouns are determined partly by whether or not the nouns are particular. If they are **not** particular in reference (*i.e.*: non-referring), a suffix -<u>i</u> is added, and it does not matter whether the speaker is talking about one or more than one item. So if you say kókkit <u>owai</u> "Give me egg(s)", in which "eggs" has the **non-particular** suffix, you may get one or more eggs; perhaps a more accurate translation would be "Give me at least one egg." Here are other examples of nouns with the non-particular suffix -<u>i</u>; notice that both animate and inanimate gender nouns take this suffix:

pookáí	"child(ren)"
í'ksisako*i*	"meat(s)"
ómahksikimii	"lake(s)"

So far as I am able to determine, nouns which are modified by a demonstrative (chapter 13) or marked for possessor (chapter 14) are always particular, *i.e.* they always refer.

Noun stems which end in non-permanent consonants <u>M</u>, <u>N</u>, or <u>S</u> (see section B above) do not retain them before the non-particular suffix -<u>i</u>:

STEM		NON-PARTICULAR FORM
máíipssiM	"belt"	máíipssii
isttoáN	"knife"	isttoáí
mo'tsíS	"hand/arm"	mo'tsíí

The non-particular and singular particular forms of many inanimate gender nouns are identical. The explanation for this is as follows. As seen in section B, inanimate gender nouns which are particular in reference add a suffix -yi when singular:

owááyi "egg"   nookóówayi "my home"

After consonants, y is lost, and what remains of the suffix -yi is identical in shape to the non-particular suffix -i just discussed. Consequently, all stems which end in permanent consonants have singular and non-particular forms which are not distinguishable; e.g.:

óóhkotoki   "stone (particular or non-particular)"
mo'tokááni "head (particular or non-particular)"

But stems which end in M, N, and S have singular forms which differ from their non-particular forms because M, N, and S are retained before the singular suffix (the y of the singular suffix is lost as after other consonants):

STEM		SINGULAR	NON-PARTICULAR
asóka'siM	"jacket"	asóka'simi	asóka'sii
atsikíN	"shoe"	atsikíni	atsikíí
mo'tsíS	"hand/arm"	mo'tsísi	mo'tsíí

In **summary**: if a speaker has no particular referent in mind for a noun, a suffix -i is added; M, N, and S are not retained before this suffix. Non-particular nouns are unmarked for number.

D. MAJOR THIRD PERSON vs. MINOR THIRD PERSON

Have you ever been troubled by the ambiguity in English sentences such as this: Clyde told his son that he could help him.? When we hear such a sentence we don't know whether the speaker means for the pronoun he to refer to 'Clyde' or to 'his son'.

But in Blackfoot, the equivalent sentence would not have this ambiguity, because Blackfoot would classify 'Clyde' and 'his son' as grammatically different. This difference would be reflected in the form of the Blackfoot equivalent of that he could help him, so we would be able to tell which of these persons is subject of 'help'.

Here, roughly, is how it works: when two or more nouns of **animate gender** occur in the same sentence, only one of them can be what we will call **major third person**;[7] the others, if particular in reference (see section C above), must be demoted to **minor third person**.[8]

So if you say *e.g.*, "The man killed the deer" in Blackfoot, either 'the man' or 'the deer' must be minor third person. When the speaker has a choice, as in this example, the noun he chooses to make major third person is thereby made more prominent in that portion of the discourse.

Minor third person singular is indicated on nouns by the suffix -yi (y is lost after consonants). Here are four examples. (Subscripted numerals are used to indicate major third person$_3$ and minor third person$_4$.)

imitáá*yi*	"dog$_4$"	póósi	"cat$_4$"
aakíí*yi*	"woman$_4$"	ísski	"pail$_4$"

An important generalization to remember is that any **animate** gender noun possessed by third person is automatically minor third person; *i.e.* if an animate gender noun has a third person (grammatical) possessor, there is no choice as to which noun is demoted; it must be the possessed noun.[9] So each of the following is minor third person:

ónni	"his$_3$ father$_4$"	oksísstsi	"his$_3$ mother$_4$"
otómitaami	"his$_3$ dog$_4$"	óhki	"his$_3$ pail$_4$".

The animate singular suffix -wa discussed in section A is actually the major third person singular suffix. Here are more examples:

imitáá*wa*	"dog$_3$"	nínna	"my father$_3$",
aakíí*wa*	"woman$_3$"	ísska	"pail$_3$"
niksíss*ta*	"my mother$_3$"		

We have seen that M, N, and S are retained (as m, n, and s) before -wa; the same is true before -yi. But remember that the y and w of these suffixes are lost because they cannot remain after consonants:

---

[7]Two or more major third persons are permitted if they are conjoined, as in "The man and woman are dancing." or "I have a dog and a cat."

[8]Called 'obviative' in most literature on Algonquian languages.

[9]Possessive affixes are treated in chapter 14.

pokóN-	"ball"	pokóna	"ball$_3$"	pokóni	"ball$_4$"
moksíS-	"awl"	moksísa	"awl$_3$"	moksísi	"awl$_4$"

The pluralizer -iksi, seen in section B of this chapter, is used for both major third and minor third person.

E. SUMMARY OF SUFFIXES ON NOUNS

non-particular   -i

		animate		inanimate
		3	4	
particular	sg	-wa	-yi	-yi
	pl	-iksi	-iksi	-istsi

Note: No noun will have more than one of these suffixes at a time.

F. A USEFUL TERM: MORPHEME

Words are usually made up of indivisible parts to which a meaning or grammatical function can be assigned; the technical term for such word parts is **morpheme**. Thus each of the suffixes in section E is a morpheme, as are the stems to which they are attached such as nínaa 'man', míín 'berry', etc. We will find this term useful in later chapters.

EXERCISES

1. Fill in the blanks:

	SINGULAR	PLURAL	NON-PARTICULAR
"tipi"	niitóyisi	niitóyiistsi	_____
"song"	nínihkssini	_____	nínihkssii
"berry"	_____	míínistsi	mííni

2. Which of the following underlined nouns would **necessarily** be minor third person in the equivalent Blackfoot sentence? (Note that 'dog' is major

third person in c.)

    a. That's my <u>son</u>; he is chasing his <u>dog</u>.
    b. I told your <u>son</u> to bring his <u>friend</u>.
    c. That dog₃ bit my <u>son</u> on his left <u>leg</u> (inanimate gender).

3. Change the following nouns from major third person singular to minor third person singular:

    a. nínaawa   "man"   c. nitána   "my daughter"
    b. póósa   "cat"   d. isttoána "knife"

4. The following is a list of all the morphemes seen in the forms given as a-d of the preceding exercise; notice that in a list of morphemes, both a form (shape) and gloss (meaning or function) are provided for each one.

    nínaa   'man'   isttoáN   'knife'
    póós   'cat'   itán   'daughter'
    n-   'my'   -wa   'major third person singular (3s)'

What additional morpheme appears in your answers to exercise 3?

5. List the morphemes you see in the following words: (Note: List each morpheme only once, as was done in exercise 4.)

    póósiksi   'cats'   nínaiksi   'men'
    kitána   'your daughter' nitániksi 'my daughters'

CHAPTER THREE

Intransitive Verbs

Verbs which occur with a subject but no object are called **intransitive** verbs. For example, in English, <u>run</u>, <u>die</u>, and <u>yawn</u> are intransitive; we say that someone (their subject) did them, but not that they did them **to** anyone or anything (an object). On the other hand, <u>hit</u>, <u>kill</u>, <u>love</u> are **transitive** verbs because they take objects; *i.e.* we must hit, kill, or love someone or something. (We begin to discuss transitive verbs in chapter 7.)

A. PERSON MARKERS

Study these Blackfoot intransitive verb forms carefully:

nitáakahkayi	"I'm going home"
kitáakahkayi	"you're going home"
áakahkayiwa	"he's going home"

What portion of the first one indicates that the speaker ("I") is the subject? What portion of the second indicates addressee ("you")? And what marks major third person ("he") in the last example?

Blackfoot verbs are marked to indicate the person (*i.e.* speaker, addressee, or other) of their subjects. (Each of the examples above is a single word; the portions <u>nit</u>- and <u>kit</u>- are prefixes, while -<u>wa</u> is a suffix.)[10] The remainder of each verb (the portion common to all three of the verb forms) is the stem.

B. THE CASE OF THE UNEXPECTED <u>S</u>

Look at these examples:

nitsíítsiniki	"I related (a story)"
kitsíítsiniki	"you related"

---

[10]We will later refer to these markers interchangeably as **person affixes** or **agreement affixes**.

iitsiníkiwa   "he related"

Can we maintain our idea that nit- and kit- mark 'speaker' and 'addressee'? If we do, we are left with an extra s in these new examples. Perhaps certain verbs take nits- and kits-, while others take nit- and kit-? But compare the same verb seen above when it has an intervening prefix á- meaning 'not an instantaneous event' (later glossed 'durative'):

    nitáítsiniki   "I relate / am relating [a story]"
    kitáítsiniki   "you relate / are relating"
    áítsinikiwa   "he relates / is relating"

These examples suggest that there is some other reason for the s after nit- and kit-.

Let's look at just a bit more evidence and then the answer to our problem of the extra s will be forthcoming:

    máátáakahkayiwa(atsiksi)[11]   "he's not going home"

Comparing this word to those seen in section A, what part of this word makes it a negative statement? Now consider the negative of "relate":

    máátsitsinikiwa(atsiksi)   "he didn't relate [a story]"

There is the ubiquitous s again, this time after the negative prefix maat. Do you have a suggestion now as to its source?

If you suggested that an s intervenes whenever t is immediately followed by i, your suggestion is correct. The sequence ti never occurs in Blackfoot; whenever we would expect ti, we find instead tsi. Thus we have a hard and fast rule of Blackfoot: t + i becomes tsi.

C. 'WE' (BUT NOT YOU)

Have you ever been put in an awkward position because the person to whom you were speaking thought you were including him when you said we, while in actuality you were using we in reference only to yourself and someone else? For example, you might have said to an acquaintance, "We are invited to the Joneses tonight.", meaning only yourself and your spouse. But the one to whom you are speaking can interpret the we as including him.

Such a misunderstanding could not arise if you were speaking Blackfoot.

---

[11]The portion atsiksi in parentheses is part of the non-affirmative third person singular suffix, generally used in negatives and questions involving third person singular as subject or object; see chapter 21.

Blackfoot grammar *requires* a speaker to indicate whether or not the one to whom he or she is speaking (the **addressee**) is included in the "action". So if you want to say "We are going to their house." in Blackfoot, there are two different ways, and you must choose between them:

1. Nitáakitapoohpinnaan ookóówaawayi.
   "We (not you) will go to their house."
2. Áakitapaoo'pa ookóówaawayi.
   "We (incl. you) will go to their house."

These two types of reference which English includes in the pronoun we, but which Blackfoot distinguishes, are traditionally termed '**exclusive we**' (speaker and at least one other, but **not** the addressee(s)) and '**inclusive we**' (speaker, addressee, and perhaps others).

D. $\underline{YOU_{sg}}$ vs. $\underline{YOU_{pl}}$: A USEFUL DISTINCTION

Up until shortly after the time of Shakespeare, English distinguished singular and plural in its terms for addressees. Thus, in the nominative case, thou was used for reference to a single addressee, and ye for reference to more than one addressee or to an addressee and other(s). Some modern American English dialects make this distinction even now, using the contraction y'all for a plural.

This same distinction is an inescapable part of Blackfoot grammar. Any reference to the addressee requires a choice between singular and plural. Here are some examples showing the contrast:

	"you_{sg}" kiistówa	"you_{pl}" kiistówaawa
"eat!"	ooyít	ooyík
"I know you"	kítssksinoo	kítssksinoohpoaawa
"your mother"	kiksíssta	kiksísstoaawa

E. VERBS WITH PLURAL SUBJECTS

Plurality of verb subjects is always marked by suffixes. Compare these singular and plural forms of the verb meaning "eat".

nitáóoyi	"I'm eating"
nitáóoyihpinnaana	"we (exclusive) are eating"
áóoyo'pa	"we (inclusive) are eating"
kitáóoyi	"you (singular) are eating"
kitáóoyihpoaawa	"you (plural) are eating"

áóoyiwa	"he is eating"[12]
áóoyiyaawa	"they are eating"

Pronunciation Notes

1. Blackfoot vowels at the end of words are usually voiceless (softly whispered).

2. A short (single) vowel, unless accented, is voiceless before h̲; in fact, the vowel and the h̲ are pronounced simultaneously.[13]

3. Before voiceless vowels (produced by the 'rules' in pronunciation notes 1. and 2.), y̲ and w̲ are pronounced with a (predictable) glottal stop; *i.e.*, the vocal chords briefly interrupt the air flow right at the beginning of any y̲ or w̲ which is followed by a voiceless vowel.[14]

EXERCISES

1. Add the missing prefixes; remember the rule for "unexpected s̲":

___áyo'kaa	"you(sg) are sleeping"
___á'po'taki	"I worked"
___ipásskaa	"I danced"
___ínihki	"you(sg) sang"

2. For the following sentences and phrases, indicate whether the English **we**, **us**, or **our** is Inclusive (includes addressee) or Exclusive:

a. Let's go to town.
b. Hey, sis, (**our**) mom is calling.
c. Give that to **us**!
d. Dear, **our** daughter is still not home (husband to wife).
e. "**Our** Father,... hallowed be thy name." (a prayer)

---

[12]Though I list the meaning "he" for most singular animate third persons, "she" or "it" might be more appropriate translations at times; see chapter 2, section A.

[13]As a reader pointed out, because h̲ always assimilates to the place and rounding features of the preceding vowel, it is more accurate to say that short vowels are dropped before h̲, leaving the h̲ with their features.

[14]Because this interruption at the glottis is totally predictable, it need not be represented in the spelling of such sequences because the glottal stop does not remain in environments where the following vowel is voiced, as it would if the glottal stop were an integral part of the morpheme involved.

Intransitive Verbs

3. For the following sentences, indicate whether the you in a and b, and the addressee in c and d, is more likely kiistówa (singular) or kiistówaawa (plural):

   a. Did **you** know that our (inclusive) son just left?
   b. I saw **you** embracing.
   c. "Go **ye** into all the world and preach the gospel" (Matthew 28:19).
   d. Please marry me!

4. Translate the following into English (for verb endings, see section E of this chapter. For verb stems, see section B and exercise 1.)

    nitáyo'kaahpinnaana
    kitá'po'takihpoaawa
    kitsipásskaahpoaawa
    nitsínihkihpinnaana
    áyo'kaayaawa
    iitsiníkio'pa

CHAPTER FOUR

More on Intransitive Verbs

A. AGREEMENT

What's wrong with these English sentences?[15]

(a) * The horses runs fast.
(b) * My son play piano.
(c) * We prefers ice cream.

In the present tense, an English verb with a third person singular subject must have the suffix -s. If it is missing when there is a third person subject as in (b), a native speaker of English rejects the sentence as ungrammatical (incorrect). And if the -s is added to a verb when the subject is not third person singular as in (a) and (c), the resultant sentence is equally bad.

Requirements of this kind are termed **agreement**. Blackfoot has extensive agreement requirements. The person affixes seen on verbs in the previous chapter must, of course, agree with whatever noun is subject. For example, consider (d), shown with a morpheme-by-morpheme analysis:[16]

(d) Nohkówa ííksspitaawa.   "My son is tall."
    n-ohkó-wa iik-sspitaa-wa
    my-son-3s very-tall-3s

Here the verb has third person singular suffix -wa, in agreement with the fact that the subject is a major third person singular noun, as shown by the -wa suffix on the noun (see chapter 1, section D). If the subject were plural, requiring a different suffix on the noun (chapter 1, section B), a plural suffix would be required on the verb also, as in (e):

---

[15]An asterisk marks an ungrammatical sentence.

[16]Unlike English, Blackfoot doesn't require the subject of a sentence to precede the verb, so the order of these words could be switched.

More on Intransitive Verbs

(e) Nohkóíksi ííksspitaayaawa.   "My sons are tall."
    n-ohkó-iksi   iik-sspitaa-yaawa
    my-son-3p   very-tall-3p

Similarly, if the subject is minor third person (4), still other suffixes are required on the verb:

(f) Ohkóyi ííksspitaayináyi.   "His son is tall."
    ohko-yi   iik-sspitaa-yináyi
    his:son-4s very-tall-4s

(g) Ohkóíksi ííksspitaayaiksi.   "His sons are tall."
    ohko-iksi iik-sspitaa-yaiksi
    his:son-4p very-tall-4p

When speaker or addressee is subject there is usually no separate *word* to indicate that fact. However, it is convenient to think of there being speaker or addressee entities present as subject at a more abstract level; this permits us to explain the corresponding person affixes on the verb as agreement. For example, in this sentence,

(h) Nitáakahkayi.   "I'm going home."
    nit-áak-ahkayi
    I-will-go^home

in which the verb has person prefix <u>nit</u>-, we can say that <u>nit</u>- agrees with the subject "speaker", even though there is no actual separate word as subject.

If a speaker's or addressee's involvement is to be emphasized, then **independent pronouns** may be used, as in the next two examples:

(i) Kiistówa, kitsíítsiniki.   "*You* related (a story)."
(j) Niistówa, nitáakahkayi.   "*I* am going home".

In such cases we can simply say that emphasis of this type is expressed by using an actual word to refer to the abstract speaker or addressee as subject. (The full set of such independent pronouns will be presented in section G of chapter 14.) The required agreement between the pronoun and the verb is already taken care of by our general statements for other nouns as subject.

There are no verb agreement affixes for non-particular nouns, so *a noun must be grammatically particular in order to be the subject of a Blackfoot verb*. In cases where the subject does not refer, and hence where one might expect a non-particular noun, one finds instead a singular or plural noun:

(k) Aakííwa áwaasai'niwa.   "(Some) woman was crying."
(l) Saahkómaapiiksi áwaawahkaayaawa.   "(Some) boys are playing"

B. SUMMARY OF VERB AFFIXES

(So far we have introduced only the person affixes used on verbs found in independent clauses. Chapter 19 will discuss use of other sets of person affixes for verbs.) Here is a chart of intransitive verb agreement affixes, all of which have been exemplified above. The following abbreviations are used from this point on: 1 = first person (speaker); 2 = second person (addressee); 3 = major third person; 4 = minor third person; 21 = inclusive "we".

number → subject person	singular		plural		
1	nit-	'I'	nit-	-hpinnaana[17]	'we(excl)'
2	kit-	'you(sg)'	kit-	-hpoaawa	'you(pl)'
21[18]	-----			-o'pa	'we(incl)'
3	-wa	'he/she'		-yi[19]	'they'
4	-yini[20]	'he/she'		-yi	'they'

C. PREDICATE ADJECTIVE = VERB

The Blackfoot equivalent of what is usually called a "predicate adjective" in English is simply an intransitive verb. A few examples should clarify what is meant here:

nitsspítaa	"I'm tall"
sspitááwa	"he is tall"
kitssoká'pssi	"you are nice"
soká'pssiwa	"he is good/nice"
soká'piiwa	"it is good"
siksináttsiwa	"it[inanimate] is black"

---

[17]The final a of -hpinnaana and -o'pa is a predictable addition after an otherwise word-final consonant, rather than part of these morphemes *per se*.

[18]The 21 form is occasionally used for unspecified subject, as *e.g.* in itáíhpiyo'pa 'there's dancing going on there'.

[19]All of the '3p' examples given so far have the form -yaawa. We will see in chapter 9 that this is made up of -yi+aawa. Until then, suffice it to say that the longer form (-yaawa) is used if the subject of the verb does not follow the verb; otherwise -yi is used.

[20]We will also see in chapter 9 that the suffixes -yináyi '4s' and -yaiksi '4p', seen above in (f) and (g), are made up of -yini+áyi and -yi+aiksi, respectively. As stated in the previous note for -yaawa, use the longer forms if the subject does not follow the verb.

siksinámma	"it[animate] is black"
síkimiwa	"he[animal] is black"

Notice that for most of these verbs there are different stem shapes depending on whether the subject is of animate gender or inanimate gender; *e.g.*, soká'pii 'good' is a stem used with inanimate gender subjects, while soká'pssi 'good' is used only with animate gender subjects. (See chapter 7.) There are also stems which are used exclusively with certain semantic classes; *e.g.*, sikimi 'black' is used only of animals [excluding people]. There are many other such restrictions on stems of this type which any fluent speaker of Blackfoot will have to know. (The Dictionary will usually provide such information.)

D. PREDICATE NOMINATIVE = VERB

As we shall see in section F of chapter 18, intransitive verbs derived from nouns by addition of the suffix -yi are the functional equivalent of so-called "predicate nominatives" in English. Note the following verbs, the stems of which are derived from the noun stems beside them:

noun stem	verb form	gloss
aakíí	nítaakiiyihpinnaan	"we are women"
(n)ínaa	kitáaksinaayi	"you will be chief"

If the subject of such verbs is third person, the derivational suffix yi is not used in independent clauses (though it is used in the other paradigms, presented in chapter 19). That the noun stems are here functioning as verb stems is evident in that the usual verb affixes are used:

noun stem	verb form	gloss
(n)ínaa	nohkówa áaksinaawa	"my son will be chief"
aakíí	aakííyaawa	"they are women"
atsikíN	amostsi atsikíniaawa	"these are shoes"

E. METEOROLOGICAL VERBS

Blackfoot sentences describing weather conditions make use of verbs also. While semantically such verbs really have no subject, they occur with the third person singular suffix -wa. Here are several examples:

Ksiistoyííwa.	"It's hot."
Áísootaawa.	"It's raining."
Áakohpotaawa.	"It's going to snow."
Íksstoyiiwa.	"It's very cold."

Áísopowa. "It's windy"
Iiyíkssopowa. "It's very windy."

EXERCISES

1. Add the correct verb affixes (recall that subscript$_4$ indicates minor third person):

   a. Niistówa, _____ áakitsiniki.
   b. Kiistówa, _____ áóoyi.
   c. Nohkóíksi áóoyi_____.
   d. Kiistónnoona, áakahkay_____.
      ("we inclusive")
   e. Ónni   áakahkayi_____.
      ("his$_{3s}$ father$_{4s}$")

2. Given the a. sentences in Blackfoot, translate the b. sentences into English:

   a. Áyo'kaawa. "She is sleeping." b. Nitáyo'kaa. "_____."
   a. Nitaókska'si. "I run." b. Kitaókska'si. "_____."
   a. Kitáíssikópii. "You are resting."
       b. Nitáíssikópiihpinnaan. "_____."
   a. Áínihkiwa. "She is singing" b. Áínihkio'pa. "_____."

3. Given the a. sentences, translate the b. sentences into Blackfoot. (Pay close attention to the subscripts.)

   a. Nitáísínaaki.   "I write."
   b. _____.   "You$_{2p}$ write."
   a. Nohkówa áókstakiwa.   "My son is reading."
   b. _____.   "My sons are reading."
   a. Á'pistotakiyaawa.   "They built."
   b. _____.   "We$_{1p}$ built."

CHAPTER FIVE

Some Phonological Rules

In chapter 3, section B, we discovered that whenever Blackfoot t precedes an i, the result is tsi. Such regular and predictable results of combining morphemes into words can be described by what are called **phonological rules**. We will need several such rules in what follows. Each rule will be given a descriptive name and stated in an explicit form called a **rewrite rule**. Each rewrite rule conforms to the following format:

$A \rightarrow B / X\_Y$

This is to be read as: "A is realized as B in the environment of a preceding X and a following Y." In any given rule, the X or Y (or both) may be unspecified, *i.e.* the preceding or following environment may be irrelevant and consequently not mentioned in the rule.

Let's now see how the rule regarding the "unexpected s" would be stated:

t-Affrication[21]

$t \rightarrow ts / \_i$

In this rule, the i after the blank corresponds to the Y in the rule format. The preceding environment is irrelevant to the rule, so there is nothing corresponding to X of the format.

We have already observed the effect of the next two rules. In chapter 2, section B, we learned that long vowels are shortened before any suffix which starts with a vowel; *e.g.* nínaa +iksi → nínaiksi 'men'. This is expressed by the following rule:

---

[21]The ts produced by this rule is not really two sounds, but a complex sound called an **affricate**.

Vowel Shortening

$$V_i: \rightarrow V_i / \_ + V$$

Here V indicates any vowel, the colon (:) is used to indicate vowel length, and the plus (+) indicates a morpheme boundary.[22] The subscripts on the two V's indicate that these two V's are of the same quality; *i.e.* only the length of the vowel is affected by this rule.[23] Also in chapter 2 we observed that y and w are lost after consonants; *e.g.*, óóhkotok + yi → óóhkotoki 'rock' and póós + wa → póósa 'cat'. The following rule accounts for this loss:

Semivowel Loss

$$G \rightarrow \emptyset / C\_ , \quad \text{where } C \neq \text{'}$$

In this rule 'G' (for 'glide') represents semivowels, and '∅' is the null or "zero" symbol; C = consonant. The statement after the rule limits the preceding environment to consonants other than the glottal stop; *i.e.*, semivowels are not lost after ' (as the following examples show: áwa'yiwa 'she's pointing'; Káta'yimmíwaatsiksi? 'Did she laugh?').

The need for the next two rules will be seen when we form plurals of verb stems ending in si. Observe the following:

(a) nitáókska'si   "I run"
(b) nitáókska'sspinnaan   "we$_{1p}$ run"
(c) áókska'so'pa   "we$_{21}$ run"

Based on what we have seen in earlier chapters (see chart in section B of chapter 4), we would have expected the latter two forms to be made up of the following parts:

(b) nit + á + okska'si + hpinnaan
(c) á + okska'si + o'pa

But in (b), the sequence si+h is realised as ss, according to the following rule:

Postsibilation

---

[22]This is necessary to permit the existence of long vowels before short vowels within a morpheme; *i.e.* we want the rule to apply only when two morphemes are combined.

[23]A better formulation of the rule is possible if vowel length is represented as a feature of vowels:

$$V \rightarrow [\text{-long}] / \_ + V$$

ih → s / s_ , where i is short and unaccented

And in (c), the sequence si+o is realised as so, according to the next rule:

i-Absorption
  i → ∅ / s_V , where i is short and unaccented, and V ≠ i or I

Observe that according to the condition on the rule the i is not "absorbed" if the following vowel is i or I.[24]

The effects of the next phonological rule to be introduced are seen by comparing the following forms:

(d) nitáakahkayi   "I'm going home"
(e) áakahkayo'pa   "we$_{21}$ are going home"

Given (d), we would expect (e) to have the form áak+ahkayi+o'pa. The loss of the vowel i is due to the following rule:[25]

i-Loss
  i → ∅ / V_1y_V_2 , where i is short and unaccented, and V_2 ≠ i or I

In chapter 2 the singular and plural of ponoká 'elk' were given as ponokáwa and ponokáíksi, respectively. The stem has an inherent accent on its third vowel, as seen in the singular. Observe that in the plural, the third syllable is accented throughout; *i.e.* the accent of the á spreads to the i of the suffix. This is true not only of the vowel combinations a+i and a+o, which are generally pronounced as single sounds (see the section on diphthongs in chapter 1), but also of o+i, i+i, a+a, and o+o. For example, the inherent accent of kakkóó 'dove' spreads to the vowel of the plural suffix in kakkóíksi. Similarly, the plural of mo'tsíS 'hand' is mo'tsíístsi. The same phenomenon is observed in the combination of the durative prefix á with any verb stem which begins with a vowel. For example, see (a)-(c) above; notice that the accent of the á has spread to the o of the stem. These facts are captured in the following rule:

---

[24]See chapter 6, section B regarding the I (called "breaking I") mentioned in this and the next rule.

[25]For some speakers, i-Loss is accompanied by lengthening of V_1 if V_1 = i. For such speakers, aókstaki+yi+aawa 'they count', *e.g.*, would be realized as aókstakiiyaawa.

Accent Spread

$$V \rightarrow [+\text{accent}] / \quad V \quad + \quad \_$$
$$\phantom{V \rightarrow [+\text{accent}] / \quad } [+\text{accent}]$$

That is, a vowel at the start of a morpheme is accented if the preceding vowel is accented.

RULE INTERACTION

Before closing this chapter, it is important to point out that there can be interaction between rules, such that the environment for one rule can exist as the result of another rule; this is known as a **feeding** relation between rules. For example, the s̲ which results from t-Affrication (t-A) can serve as the environment for Postsibilation (P-s):

$$ \text{t-A} \text{P-s}$$
(f) nit+ihpiyi → nitsihpiyi → nítsspiyi "I danced"

So t-Affrication feeds Postsibilation. In general, we assume that rules interact such that there is maximal feeding; exceptions must be stated explicitly. Example (g) shows the interaction of three rules; Semivowel Loss, t-Affrication, and i-Absorption:

(g) mohkát+yi+aawa → mohkáti+aawa →
    mohkátsi+aawa → mohkátsaawa "They are feet."

When the application of one rule prevents another rule from applying, this is referred to as a **bleeding** relation between rules. In general, we assume that rules interact such that there is minimal bleeding, and exceptions must be stated. (In chapter 14 (second paragraph) we will see examples in which the very nature of pairs of rules precludes both rules applying; consequently, which rule bleeds the other must be stated.)

Supplemental Material

The reader may have noted that i-Absorption and i-Loss are very similar. Yet as they stand they cannot be combined into a single rule, for i-Loss requires a preceding vowel and i-Absorption does not. However, the major purpose of the requirement that the y̲ in i-Loss be preceded by a vowel is to assure that when the sequence y̲iV follows a consonant, as in miin+yi+aawa 'they are berries', the y̲ is lost by Semivowel Loss, and the i̲ remains. If the applicational precedence of Semivowel Loss were otherwise assured (by a statement that Semivowel Loss bleeds i-Loss), then i-Loss could be stated without requiring the presence of a vowel before the y̲. This would allow collapsing of i-Loss and i-Absorption into one rule, call it **i-Drop**: $i \rightarrow \emptyset / \{y,s\}\_V$, where V ≠ i or I.

Some Phonological Rules

However, this course of action is not attractive, because y and s do not form a natural class, and the two rules, i-Absorption and i-Loss, seem to describe separate phenomena. The latter is evident in the case of speakers for whom i-Loss, but not i-Absorption, is accompanied by lengthening of a preceding i; see footnote 25. So i-Absorption and i-Loss are kept as separate rules in this work.

EXERCISES

1. The stem for 'sleep' is yo'kaa. (See exercise 2 of chapter 4.) When the prefix á (to be discussed in chapter 6) is added, the result is the 'durative' stem, which usually translates as 'be sleeping'. How would 'we$_{21}$ are sleeping' (durative) be written? What phonological rule applies?

2. The stem for 'count/read' is okstaki; 'she is counting' is áókstakiwa, and includes the durative prefix. What phonological rule has applied in this word?

3. Given: nitáókska'si 'I run/ I'm running', nitókska'si 'I ran'. Observe that here, as with many verbs of Blackfoot, removal of the prefix á (called the 'durative' in chapter 6) results in a past tense translation into English. We saw in exercise 2 of chapter 4 that 'she is singing' is áínihkiwa. How would you write 'I sang' in Blackfoot? What phonological rule applies?

4. Given: áó'tsisiiwa 'she smokes (tobacco)'. How would 'we$_{21}$ are smoking' be written? Besides Accent Spread, two phonological rules apply, and in a certain order. What are they? (Remember that double vowels represent long vowels.)

CHAPTER SIX

Tense and Aspect

A. PRELUDE: TENSE vs ASPECT

To begin this chapter, we will discuss the definitions of the terms 'tense' and 'aspect', using examples from English even though tense and aspect categories of Blackfoot do not find an exact match in English.

Tense can be described roughly as an indication of the **time** of an event or process relative to the time of the utterance of the sentence in which tense is indicated. For example, in the sentence <u>Bill</u> <u>ran</u> <u>to</u> <u>the store.</u>, the past tense of the verb <u>run</u> indicates that Bill's running took place prior to the time at which the speaker is uttering the sentence. Similarly, in <u>Bill</u> <u>will</u> <u>run</u> <u>to</u> <u>the store.</u>, the use of the auxiliary verb <u>will</u> indicates that the speaker expects the event to take place subsequent to the time at which the sentence is uttered, *i.e.* in the future. **Aspect**, on the other hand, involves indication of the **degree of completion** of an event or process at the time of the utterance or relative to some specified reference point in time.[26]

Aspect in English is indicated in combination with tense. For example, in <u>Bill</u> <u>is</u> <u>running.</u>, the use of the auxiliary verb <u>be</u> plus the suffix <u>ing</u> on <u>run</u> indicates that Bill's running is going on (uncompleted) at the time of the utterance. The fact that this continuous aspect is relative to the time of the utterance is signalled by the use of a present tense form (<u>is</u>) of the verb <u>be</u>. This becomes evident when we compare the following sentence with a past tense form of the verb <u>be</u>: <u>Bill</u> <u>was</u> <u>running</u> <u>when</u> <u>I</u> <u>saw</u> <u>him</u> <u>yesterday.</u>; notice that here the continuous aspect is described relative to the point in time when the event was observed.

---

[26]Discussion of tense and aspect requires division of verbs into at least three types: those which describe **processes**, those which describe **events** (processes which naturally or conventionally reach an end point), and those which describe **states**. Discussion in this chapter will be limited to indication of tense and aspect on process and eventive verbs.

Tense and Aspect

In Blackfoot, tense and aspect are indicated by prefixes which are part of verb stems. That is, they combine with simpler stems to form complex stems. Consequently, tense or aspect prefixes never precede person agreement prefixes.

B. FUTURE TENSE

Future tense in Blackfoot is marked by prefix yáak-,[27] as seen in the following examples:[28]

(a) Oma saahkómaapiwa áaka'po'takiwa.   "The boy will work."
    om-wa saahkómaapi-wa yáak-a'po'taki-wa
    that-3s boy-3s fut-work-3s

(b) Nitáakitsiniki.   "I will tell a story."
    nit-yáak-itsiniki
    1-fut-relate

(c) Kitáaksipii.   "You will enter."
    kit-yáak-Ipii
    2-fut-enter

The s following the future prefix in (c) requires some discussion. The initial vowel of stem ipii 'enter', unlike the initial vowel of itsiniki 'tell a story', always causes a preceding k to be replaced by the affricate ks. We will speak of this phenomenon as **breaking** of k, and of the i which is involved as a **breaking i**. For any morpheme which begins with i we need to know whether that i is a breaking i or not; if it is a breaking i, then if it is placed next to a morpheme ending in k we know that the k will be replaced by ks.[29] When wishing to represent the difference between a breaking i and a non-breaking i

---

[27]Because of Semivowel Loss (introduced in the preceding chapter) and Semivowel Drop (to be introduced in chapter 14) the y of this morpheme will show up only after a morpheme which ends in a vowel (as in (r) below) or glottal stop.

[28]From this point on, where it seems useful an interlinear, morpheme-by-morpheme analysis of examples will be included, even though in some cases that analysis will involve grammatical devices which are not discussed until later. Note that in the morpheme analysis, word spaces and hyphens in the Blackfoot line correspond to spaces and hyphens in the gloss line, so that morpheme shapes can be matched up to their glosses even though glosses may not be directly under them.

[29]For this reason, nearly every morpheme listed in the Blackfoot Dictionary which begins with i is accompanied by a diagnostic example in which the i in question is preceded by a morpheme ending in k.

There are other ways in which a breaking i affects its environment differently than non-breaking i, but these involve details of analysis which will get little attention in this description.

in this book, we will represent the former with a capital I̲. So in a listing of the stems for 'enter' and 'tell a story', the former would begin with I̲ (as it does in the morpheme-by-morpheme representation in (c) above) and the latter with i̲. And to the phonological rules presented thus far, we add the following:

Breaking

    k → ks / _I

The representation which involves I̲ versus i̲ is more abstract than the usual spelling system for Blackfoot; in the latter, both I̲ and i̲ are represented by i̲ because they are realized (pronounced) as the same sound. So in addition to the rule of Breaking, we need a rule which says that the difference between these two vowels is neutralized at the level of pronunciation. This is what the following rule does, in effect:

Neutralization

    I → i

In addition to future prefix yáak, there is a related prefix áyaak "imminent future" (i.fut):[30]

(d) Nitáyaakihpiyi.   "I'm about to dance."
    nit-áyaak-ihpiyi
    1-i.fut-dance

(e) Anná pookáawa áyaakasai'niwa.   "That child is about to cry."
    ann-wa pookáá-wa áyaak-wa:sai'ni-wa[31]
    that-3s child-3s i.fut-cry-3s

C. DURATIVE ASPECT

The description of an event or process can include indication that it is on-going or continuous by use of prefix á 'durative'.[32]

---

[30] It is conceivable that this is a combination of the durative prefix (see below) and the future prefix, but since not all speakers distinguish yáak- and áyaak-, such an analysis is difficult to defend.

[31] See section B of chapter 15 regarding the vowel a:.

[32] Glossed as 'not an instantaneous event' in chapter 3.

Tense and Aspect

(f) Nóko'siksi áyimmiyaawa.   "My kids are laughing."
    n-oko's-iksi á-yImmi-yi-aawa
    1-offspring-3p dur-laugh-3p-PRO[33]

(g) Omiksi pookáíksi áwaawahkaayaawa.   "Those children are playing."
    om-iksi pookáá-iksi á-wa:wahkaa-yi-aawa
    that-3p child-3p   dur-play-3p-PRO

Prefixes which end in <u>a</u> form diphthongs[34] with a following <u>i</u> or <u>o</u>, and the inherent accent of the durative prefix is realized on the diphthong; but since the diphthongs are spelled as a sequence of two vowels, the accent is indicated on both, as seen in (h) and (i). The rule of Accent Spread (chapter 5) accounts for this.

(h) Omá síípisttowa áípottaawa.   "The owl is flying."
    om-wa síípistto-wa á-Ipottaa-wa
    that-3s owl-3s   dur-fly-3s

(i) Nitáókska'si.   "I run. / I'm running."
    nit-á-okska'si
    1-dur-run

For verb stems which begin with the prefix <u>a'p</u> 'around, about', the durative prefix is placed after the <u>a'p</u>.[35]

(j) Nitá'pao'taki   "I work."
    nit-a'p-á-o'taki
    1-PREF-dur-work

Durative aspect may be used with future tense, as seen in (k):

(k) Apinákosi áakaokska'so'pa.   "Tomorrow we$_{21}$ will be running."
    apinákosi yáak-a-okska'si-o'pa
    tomorrow   fut-dur-run-21

---

[33]See chapter 9 regarding PRO.

[34]See chapter 1.

[35]The combination of <u>a'p</u> with other stems often is a "frozen" form which is not currently recognized as a combination of morphemes. E.g. a'po'taki 'work', seen in (j), is analyzable as <u>a'p</u> + <u>o'taki</u> 'take', but the meaning of the combination is not predictable from the meanings of the parts. In such cases <u>a'p</u> will be glossed simply 'PREF' and the remainder of the stem will be glossed with the meaning of the combination.

Supplemental Material

Though it is not so-written in this book, the vowel of the durative is probably long when in the first syllable of a word, when preceded only by a person agreement prefix, or if preceded by the vowel i; see the discussion of "variable length" vowels in chapter 15. The apparent inherent accent of this morpheme in the same positions is probably the result of its underlying length, for accent assignment rules, though poorly understood, are clearly sensitive to syllable structure, including length of vowels.

Also, this morpheme apparently begins with y when preceded by a morpheme which ends in a glottal stop; see example (h) of chapter 21.

D. PERFECTIVE ASPECT

Indication that an event is completed or a process has terminated before the present or other specified reference point in time, is indicated by means of prefix ákaa, as seen in the following:

(l) Anníksi aakííkoaiksi ákaayo'kaayaawa.   "Those girls have slept."
    ann-iksi aakííkoaN-iksi ákaa-yo'kaa-yi-aawa
      that-3p   girl-3p   perf-sleep-3p-PRO

(m) Amo nínaawa ákaa'paistotakiwa náápioyii.[36]
    amo nínaa-wa ákaa-a'p-a-istotaki-wa náápioyiS-i
    that man-3s perf-PREF-dur-make(AI) house-nonpartic
"This man has built a house."

The perfective prefix has the form shown above only when at the beginning of a word. If preceded by another prefix, it has the variant form Ikaa-, as seen in (n)-(p):

(n) Anná saahkómaapiiwa máátsikáíhpiyiwa.   "The boy hasn't danced."
    ann-wa saahkómaapii-wa máát-Ikaa-ihpiyi-wa
      that-3s   boy-3s   neg-perf-dance-3s

(o) Nikáó'toohpinnaan.   "We have arrived."
    n-Ikaa-o'too-hpinnaan
    1-perf-arrive-1p

---

[36] The stem for 'build' here also has the durative prefix, possibly to indicate it is the building *process* which is completed. An alternative explanation may be that all verb stems which begin with a'p- require the durative with the perfective prefix; I have found no evidence to the contrary.

(p) Kikááyimmi. "You have laughed."
    k-Ikaa-yImmi
    2-perf-laugh

The last two examples require discussion. Based on what has been presented thus far, the reader should be wondering why (o) and (p) do not begin with nit and kit. Simply stated, certain morphemes select a short form of preceding person agreement prefixes nit-, kit-, and ot-; the corresponding short variants are n-, k-, and w-. One must learn which morphemes, like Ikaa, select the short forms of these agreement prefixes. Also, since the non-initial form of the perfective prefix is shown to start with breaking I, we need to account for the fact that the second person prefix k is not "broken" in (p). It turns out that the k of the second person prefix is always impervious to Breaking.

The perfective prefix may be used with the future tense prefix, as seen in (q) and (r); note that the relative order of these prefixes is significant:

(q) Apinákosi áaksíkaoka'pihtsiiyiwa. "Tomorrow it will have spoiled."
    apinákosi yáak-Ikaa-oka'pihtsiiyi(II)-wa
    tomorrow   fut-perf-spoil(II)-3s

(r) Ákaayáakaniiwa. "He *will* be saying that."
    ákaa-yáak-wa:nii-wa
    perf-fut-say(AI)-3s

The use of the perfective in this last example seems to reflect certainty of the speaker.[37]

E. PAST TENSE

This is the most complicated of the tense and aspect morphemes because its discussion involves the area of greatest irregularity in Blackfoot: morpheme-initial variation. Consequently, the presentation here will be incomplete and somewhat oversimplified. (Morpheme-initial variation will be discussed more fully in chapter 15.)

Past tense is realized in several variant forms, depending upon the following factors: whether or not an agreement prefix is present, properties of the first morpheme of the stem, and, when competing forms exist, preference or dialect of the speaker.

Past tense may be realized as any of the following (examples will follow as

---

[37] According to Greg Thomson (personal communication), the combination of ákaa and yáak is an idiom, *i.e.* is a single lexical item with a meaning that is not predictable if viewed simply as a combination of these two morphemes. Given that analysis, my statement above about the relative order of these morphemes is misleading.

(s) - (z)):

1. Simple absence of both the durative aspect and future prefixes, often with placement of accent on a syllable that otherwise would not be accented;[38]

2. Replacement of a stem-initial vowel by ii, or, if the stem begins in a consonant, addition of an ii, usually long, before that consonant;[39]

3. For a small subset of stems beginning with sV or ICV [where C and V stand for any consonant and vowel], replacement of this initial sequence by sayV or CayV, respectively; this is possible only in word-initial position (*i.e.* when no prefix precedes the stem). We will refer to this process as **initial change**. (Initial change is also found in some imperative forms and a few nominalized verbs.)[40]

4. In the Blackfoot Reserve dialect only, there is a fourth way of marking past tense on stems, but only if they are in word-initial position: Add prefix ná.

For most verbs, there is more than one acceptable way of indicating past tense on some forms from the agreement paradigm.

Here are examples of various past tense forms, identified in square brackets as to whether they illustrate type 1, 2, 3, or 4. Notice that for many verbs there are two or three acceptable past tense forms:

(s) Nitókska'si [1] / Nitsííkska'si [2].   "I ran."
(t) Nohkówa ííkska'siwa [2]/ **ná**ókska'siwa [4].   "My son ran."
(u) Oma píítaawa ipóttaawa [1] / p**ay**óttaawa [3] / **ná**ípottaawa [4].
    "The eagle flew."
(v) Kitána aasáí'niwa [1].   "Your daughter cried."
(w) Amo aakííwa **ii**hpómmaawa [2] ónnikii.   "This woman bought milk."
(x) Nítsspiyihpinnaan [1].   "We danced."

The past tense morpheme is usually realized on the first syllable of the verb

---

[38]It is not yet clear whether the accent placement in such cases is a function of the past tense itself, or a consequence of the absence of any prefix with inherent accent.

[39]This means of marking past tense is never possible for stems beginning with a'p.

[40]Some of the cases of initial ii described in 2. are apparently also cognate with the process known as initial change in other Algonquian languages (see Taylor 1967), but in this description we will reserve the term for the process described in 3.

after the agreement prefix, if any. So if it appears with perfective aspect, the perfective prefix is affected:

(y) Oma imitááwa ííkáóoyiwa [2].   "That dog had eaten."

Notice also that the non-initial variant of the perfective prefix is used, suggesting that at least with regard to variant selection, the past tense morpheme is a prefix. This can also account for the fact that although the perfective prefix otherwise selects the short form of the person agreement prefixes, the past tense does not; so 'past' plus 'perfect' selects the long form:

(z) **Kit**sííkaokstoohp(.yi [2].   "You (pl) had read it."

EXERCISES

Note: All verb stems and noun phrases needed for the following exercises can be found in the current chapter.

1. Translate the following into Blackfoot, using the future tense morphemes:

(a) Your daughter is about to run.

(b) (The) owls will fly.

(c) I will build a house. [Note: Prefix <u>a'p</u> 'around, about' is part of the stem for 'build/make'. See example (m) above.]

2. Translate the following, using the durative aspect morpheme:

(a) This woman is laughing.

(b) My kids are sleeping.

(c) I am telling a story.

3. Translate the following, using the perfective aspect morpheme:

(a) We$_{1p}$ have run.

(b) This man has told a story.

(c) You$_{2s}$ have flown.

CHAPTER SEVEN

Four Verb Stem Types

A. SYNTAX

Constraints on the way words combine into larger constructions such as phrases, clauses, and sentences, are referred to as "syntactic constraints" or "rules of syntax". Such rules describe requirements which must be met when words are combined, such as their grammatical class, morphological makeup, and their relative order. We have already seen in chapter 4 that verbs must agree with their subjects; this is an example of a syntactic constraint, for it restricts what the morphological makeup of the verb can be, based on the nominal (noun or noun phrase) as its subject.

Although there will be no chapter entitled "syntax" in this book, and the word syntax will not appear often, rules of syntax will be met in just about every chapter. The remainder of this chapter deals with three syntactic topics.

B. VERB STEM TYPES and STEM AGREEMENT

In chapter 4, section C, we saw that Blackfoot intransitive verb stems which take animate gender subjects usually have different shapes than stems which take inanimate gender subjects. The examples are repeated here:

soká'pssiwa	"he is good/nice"
soká'piiwa	"it[inanimate] is good"
siksinámma	"it[animate] is black"
siksináttsiwa	"it[inanimate] is black"

We describe this situation by saying that the verb subcategory 'Intransitive Verb' is further subcategorized according to the grammatical gender of the subject. Following traditional Algonquianist terminology, we will refer to the two subcategories of intransitive verb stems as Animate Intransitive (AI) and Inanimate Intransitive (II). There are also two subcategories of transitive verbs. (Recall that transitive verbs take objects.) The two subcategories of transitive verbs are distinguished according to whether their objects are animate or inanimate gender, and are referred to as Transitive Animate (TA) and Transitive Inanimate (TI).[41] The selection of verb stem type according to gender of the subject or object is often referred to as **stem agreement**. From this point on, we will use this term when refering to choice of verb stem. (The phrase **verb agreement** will then refer to inflectional agreement, as elaborated in the following section.)

In summary, the two parameters of verb subcategorization, namely transitivity and gender, combine to produce four stem types:

	Animate	Inanimate
Intransitive	AI	II
Transitive	TA	TI

In the Dictionary, the four types of verb stems are labeled as *vai, vii, vta,* and *vti.*

C. INFLECTIONAL AGREEMENT

We have seen in previous chapters (especially chapter 4) that intransitive verbs take affixes which must agree with the subjects of the verbs to which they are attached. The agreement affixes which occur on intransitive verbs of independent clauses were summarized in section B of chapter 4. The set of affixes presented there is for AI verbs. The affixes found on II verbs are a subset of the AI affixes, limited by the fact that the only inanimate gender categories are singular and plural; *i.e.* **the set of II agreement affixes has only 3s and 3p forms, and these are identical to the 3s and 3p forms for AI verbs** given in section B of chapter 4.

Transitive verbs of Blackfoot take affixes which agree with their subjects and their objects. Notice that the following four sentences all have different verb forms as a consequence of the fact that no two have the same combination of subject and object:

(a) Niistówa, ***nit***ohpómmatoohp***a*** amoyi náápioyisi.

"*I* bought this house."

---

[41] All transitive verbs of Blackfoot require subjects capable of acting willfully. Consequently, transitive verbs are not subcategorized in terms of gender of their subject, since such referents automatically belong to the animate gender class. We will see in chapters 8 (last section) and 12 (section D) how Blackfoot expresses things like "A shoe broke the glass." and "The stick hit me."

(b) Kiistówa, *kit*ohpómmatoohp*a* amoyi náápioyisi.
"*You* bought this house."

(c) Niistówa, *nit*ohpómmatoohp*i* amo(i)stsi náápioyiistsi.
"*I* bought these houses."

(d) Kiistówa, *kit*ohpómmatoohp*i* amo(i)stsi náápioyiistsi.
"*You* bought these houses."

The verbs in these examples are transitive inanimate (TI). The full set of agreement forms for TI verbs in independent clauses will be given in the next chapter. The agreement forms for transitive animate (TA) verbs in independent clauses will be presented in chapters 10, 11, and 12.

D. OBJECTS THAT DON'T COUNT

If an object is either unspecified as in (e) and (f), or non-particular in reference (see chapter 2, section C) as in (g) and (h), it does not qualify as a primary syntactic object, and the verb of which it is the logical object will be inflectionally intransitive. Consequently, the verbs of (e)-(h) are AI rather than TI; compare the verb of (e) and (g) to the TI form in (a) above:

(e) Nítohpommaa. "I purchased (something unspecified)."
(f) Áwaaniiwa. "He's saying (something)."
(g) Nítohpommaa náápioyii. "I made a house-purchase."
(h) Áóoyiyaawa owáí. "They are eating egg(s)."

Objects with which verbs do not agree will be referred to as **secondary objects**.

Supplemental Material

We have seen that there are two criteria for determining the transitivity of verbs in Blackfoot: syntactic and morphological. Syntactic transitivity is the ability to occur with an object, while morphological transitivity is the ability to show inflectional agreement with an object. Where these two criteria conflict, we will use the prefix "para-" to modify the syntactic category of the verb. So AI verbs which may occur with a non-particular object will be referred to as **paratransitive**,[42] because they may occur with objects but do not agree with those objects.

There are also two types of TA verbs. Some TA verbs may occur with two syntactic objects, but the verb will show inflectional agreement with only one of

---

[42]Such verbs were referred to as 'pseudo-intransitive' in Frantz (1970). Taylor (1969) introduced the latter term for a derived morphological class, but his discussion (p.165) makes it clear that such a category is necessary for syntax as well.

them, which we will call the **primary object**. Such verbs can then be referred to as **paraditransitive** verbs, because although they are syntactically ditransitive (take two objects), they are inflectionally (mono)transitive, since they show inflectional agreement with only the primary object. The other object, which we will call the **secondary object**, may be either particular or non-particular in reference. We will have reason to make use of these new terms, 'paratransitive' and 'paraditransitive', in chapter 20.

EXERCISE

If translating the following sentences into Blackfoot, would the Blackfoot verb stem required be II, AI, TI, or TA? (If you are uncertain about the grammatical gender of the nouns involved, see chapter 2.)

1. I'm working.

2. The tipi is old.

3. He's eating the meat.

4. I found the pail.

5. We bought fish (non-particular).

6. The horse is eating.

CHAPTER EIGHT

Transitive Inanimate Verbs

A complete set of agreement forms for a verb is called a **paradigm**. Observe the following paradigm for TI verb stem ikooni 'take down (gently)'. It is divided here into two portions; the first is used with a singular object and the second with a plural object.

Singular object forms:

Subject number → person	singular	plural
1	nitsííkooniihpa	nitsííkooniihpinnaana
2	kitsííkooniihpa	kitsííkooniihpoaawa
21	---------	ikóónii'pa
3	ikóónima	ikóónimi
4	ikóónimini	ikóónimi

Plural object forms:

Subject number → person	singular	plural
1	nitsííkooniihpi	nitsííkooniihpinnaani
2	kitsííkooniihpi	kitsííkooniihpoaayi
21	---------	ikóónii'pi
3	ikóónima	ikóónimi
4	ikóónimini	ikóónimi

There are a number of things to notice about this paradigm. First, as will be even more obvious when the affixes of this paradigm are listed separately below, there is a great deal of similarity between this paradigm and the AI paradigm given in section B of chapter 4. Second, comparing the singular object forms with the plural object forms, we see that if the subject is 3 or 4 the two sets of forms are the same (i.e. number of the object is not indicated in the verb) whereas forms with other subjects end in a (from -wa) if the object is singular and with i (from -yi) if the object is plural. The forms with 3 or 4 as subject form a subset in another regard, as well; they have im where the others have iihp. This is true for all TI verbs, though many have oom and oohp in place of im and iihp.[43] Because all TI verbs show this hp ~ m[44] variation in the independent paradigm, we will refer to this portion as a **TI theme** suffix. All speakers find 'p in place of hp to be perfectly acceptable in this paradigm.

Here are some sentences utilizing forms from the above paradigm:

(g) Nohkówa ikóónima ómi niitóyisi.   "My son took down that tipi."

(h) Kohkóíksi ikóónimi(aawa) ánni nitsiksíkkokóówayi.

"Your sons took my tent down."

(i) Ikóónii'pi ómistsi ksíkkokóówaistsi.   "Those tents were taken down."

(j) Áaksikoonii'pa oyísi.   "We$_{21}$ will take down his lodge."

THE TI THEME SUFFIXES AND AGREEMENT AFFIXES

Subject number → person	singular		plural	
1	nit-	-hp	nit-	-hpinnaan
2	kit-	-hp	kit-	-hpoaa
21/unspec[45]	-----		-'p	
3	-mwa		-myi	
4	-myini		-myi	

The following points require explanation or bear repeating:

1. Theme suffix hp in this paradigm may be replaced by 'p.

2. Theme suffixes hp and 'p in this paradigm lengthen a preceding

---

[43]TI stems are listed in the Dictionary as ending in i, ii, or oo. The length of the vowel is relevant in other than the independent paradigm.

[44]For a great many speakers, this is hp ~ mm. So, for example, the verb of (g) will frequently be heard as ikóónimma.

[45]The 21 form is also used for unspecified subject, as seen in (i) above, which is more literally translated "Unspecified took those tents down."

short vowel.

3. Theme suffix m in the 3 and 4 portions of this paradigm shortens a preceding long ii.[46]

4. Semivowel Loss eliminates the w and y of the 3 and 4 forms;[47] see chapter 5.

5. To these affixes are added -wa if the object is singular or -yi if the object is plural, *unless* the subject is 3 or 4; in the latter cases number of the object is not indicated in the verb due to the following general constraints of Blackfoot: Verbs can agree with only one 3rd person nominal, and animate gender takes precedence over inanimate gender when there is a choice.

TI WITH INANIMATE LOGICAL SUBJECT

Transitive verbs of Blackfoot require subjects which are animate, and this animacy apparently must be real, *i.e.* it is not a gender requirement but a requirement that the subject must reference an entity which is capable of exercising will. So, for example, even though isttoáN 'knife' is of animate gender, it cannot serve as subject of a transitive verb, and the following sentence is unacceptable:[48]

(k) * Oma isttoána ikahksínima annistsi ikkstsíksiistsi.

("That knife cut off those branches.")

Instead of translating such sentences literally, Blackfoot requires use of the unspecified subject form of the verb (the same as the 21 subject form); the (unwillfull) involvement of the logical subject is expressed by use of the "linking" prefix iiht 'means' (see section 4 of chapter 16), as seen in the following example:

(l) Oma isttoána **iiht**síkahksinii'pi annistsi ikkstsíksiistsi.

"The knife cut off those branches."

A more literal translation of (l) is "By means of the knife, the branches were cut off."

---

[46]Though there are a few apparent exceptions in the Dictionary; *e.g.* TI verb sta'toksii 'split (wood)'; note áakssta'toksiimáyi 'he will split it'.

[47]These semivowels are included in the chart so that the similarity between the TI and AI paradigms will be evident.

[48]Unless in a context in which the knife is personified, in which case the stated requirement of willful action is met.

EXERCISES

1. Comparing the chart on page 43 with that on page 22, list the ways in which the TI paradigm differs from the AI paradigm.

2. Add the correct TI affixes to the verbs in the following sentences. (The verb stem is in first position in each sentence given, except for j., where it is in second position.)

    a.   áakohpommatoo   amo nínaawa omi napayíni
         "The man will buy that bread."

    b.   áakohpommatoo   omistsi ápssiistsi
         "I will buy those arrows."

    c.   áakohpommatoo   amoyi sóópa'tsisi
         "We$_{21}$ will buy this chair."

    d.   áóowatoo   omistsi ókonokistsi
         "You$_{2p}$ are eating those saskatoons."

    e.   áyoohtsi   anniksi aakííksi omi nínihkssini
         "Those women hear the song."

    f.   áókstoo   nóko'siksi omistsi náápioyiistsi
         "My kids are counting those houses."

    g.   áápiksii   omiksi pookáíksi omistsi óóhkotokistsi
         "Those kids threw those rocks."

    h.   máátakohkottsipikkstsi   ohkóyi amoyi i'ksisakoyi
         "His son can't chew this meat."

    i.   iini   kookóówayi
         "We$_{1p}$ saw your house."

    j.   nookóówayi   áwa'yihkihtsi   omi ápssiyi
         "That arrow is pointing at my house."
         [Hint: See discussion of examples (k) and (l) above.]

CHAPTER NINE

Attached Pronouns

Certain third person suffixes appear to have a longer form than that listed in the charts given so far. For example, the charts list -yi as '3p', yet in section A of chapter 4 the following example was given; note the highlighted portion:

(a) Nohkóíksi ííksspitaa*yaawa*.   "My sons are tall."

But if the subject nohkóíksi is placed after the verb rather than before it, we see the suffix -yi :

(b) Ííksspitaa*yi* nohkóíksi.   "My sons are tall."

And only the form with yaawa is acceptable if there is no overt noun or noun phrase as subject in the clause:

(c) Ííksspitaa*yaawa*.   "They are tall."

So it seems that the "long" form is required if a noun with which it agrees does not follow the verb. This suggests an analysis in which the longer form of the 3p ending involves a third person pronoun aawa which attaches to the end of the verb,[49] immediately after the suffix -yi. (The i of -yi is lost in (a) and (c) according to the rule called **i-Loss**; see chapter 5.)

The above example involved a pronoun as subject of an AI verb; here is an example of the pronoun aawa as object of a TI verb:

(d) Nitohpómmatoo'p*aawa*.   "I bought them."
    nit-ohpommatoo-'p-yi-aawa
    1-buy(TI)-theme-ip-PRO

Note that because the inanimate plural ('ip') suffix -yi in (d) follows a consonant, i-Loss does not apply but Semivowel Loss does; consequently the i of -yi shows up.

---

[49] Such pronouns are commonly known as **enclitic** pronouns.

There is also an attached pronoun for third person singular, but it is used only when there is another third person in the immediate context, though not necessarily in the same sentence. We will refer to this pronoun as the **Distinct Third Person (DTP)** pronoun. Here are some examples:

(e) Nohkówa áakohpommatoomáyi.　　　　　"My son will buy it."
　　n-ohkó-wa yáak-ohpommatoo-m-wa-áyi
　　1-son-3s fut-buy(TI)-theme-3s-PRO

(f) Ánna aakííwa óomi ápao'takiyináyi.
　　ann-wa aakííwa w-óom-yi a'pao'taki-yini-áyi
　　that-3s woman-3s 3-husband-4s work(dur)-4s-PRO
　　"That woman's husband is working."

(g) Otsáápioyisi,　ksikksináttsiwáyi.　　　　"His house is white."
　　ot-Iáápioyis-yi ksikksinattsi-wa-áyi
　　3-house-in.s[50]　white-in.s-PRO

The pronoun in these examples is evidently <u>áyi</u>, and if the segment preceding this pronoun is a vowel, that vowel is deleted.

There are plural DTP pronouns, as well; one for animate gender nominals and the other for inanimate gender nominals; these are <u>aiksi</u> and <u>aistsi</u>, respectively. These require deletion of a preceding <u>a</u> (as in (h) and (l)), and also require deletion of a preceding <u>i</u> if it in turn is preceded by <u>m</u> or <u>n</u> (as in (k)). Here are several examples:

(h) Nohkówa áakohpommatoomaistsi.　　　"My son will buy them."
　　n-ohkó-wa yáak-ohpommatoo-m-wa-aistsi
　　1-son-3s fut-buy(TI)-theme-3s-PRO

(i) Otsáápioyiistsi ksikksináttsiyaistsi.　　　"His houses are white."
　　ot-Iáápioyis-istsi ksikksinattsi-yi-aistsi
　　3-house-ip　white-ip-PRO

(j) Óko'siksi　áyo'kaayaiksi.　　　　　　"His kids are sleeping."
　　w-óko's-iksi á-Io'kaa-yi-aiksi
　　3-offspring-4p dur-sleep-4p-PRO

(k) Anni óomi á'pistotsiminaistsi.　　　　　"Her husband made them."
　　ann-yi w-óom-yi á'pistotsi-m-yini-aistsi
　　that-4s 3-husband make(TI)-theme-4s-PRO

---

[50]'in.s' in morpheme-by-morpheme glosses abbreviates 'inanimate singular'.

(l) Anna pookááwa iinoyííwaiksi.   "That child saw them (anim)."
    ann-wa pookáá-wa iino-yii-wa-aiksi
    that-3s child-3s past:see-dir-3s-PRO

Attached pronouns can bear grammatical relations other than subject or object. Here are examples as destinational Goal, Instrument, and Location:[51]

(m) Nitákkawa itápsskonakiwaiksi.   "My friend shot at them (anim)."
    n-itákka-wa itap-sskonaki-wa-aiksi
    1-friend-3s toward-shoot-3s-PRO

(n) Kitána iihtáóoyiwáyi.   "Your daughter is eating with it."
    k-itán-wa iiht-á-ooyi-wa-áyi
    2-daughter-3s instr-dur-eat(AI)-3s-PRO

(o) Oma aakííkoana itohkítopiiwaistsi.   "That girl sat on them (inan)."
    om-wa aakííkoaN-wa it-ohkit-opii-wa-aistsi
    that-3s girl-3s there-upon-sit-3s-PRO

Two pronouns may be attached to a verb, but the two must be different. The constraints involved in such cases are fairly complex,[52] but the following rules cover most circumstances:

1. At least one of the two pronouns must reference the subject or object.

2. If one of the pronouns is subject or object and the other is not subject or object, the pronoun as subject or object is closest to the stem.

3. If one pronoun is major third person (3) and the other is minor third person (4), the 3 pronoun precedes the 4 pronoun (no matter which is subject).

4. The two pronouns must not be identical. In cases where two identical pronouns are called for, only one will be present.

Here are examples with two pronouns:

(p) Nohkóíksi áakohpommatoomiaawaistsi. "My sons will buy them."
    n-ohkó-iksi yáak-ohpommatoo-m-yi-aawa-aistsi
    1-son-3p fut-buy(TI)-theme-ip-PRO-PRO

---

[51] See section D.4 of chapter 16 for discussion of how these relations are indicated in Blackfoot.

[52] See Fox and Frantz 1979 for details.

(q) Anni otáni, itohkítopiiyináyaiksi
ann-yi w-itan-yi it-ohkit-opii-yini-áyi-aiksi
that-in.s 3-da.-4s there-on-sit-4s-PRO-PRO
"His daughter, she sat on them(anim)."

SUMMARY

If a noun bearing a grammatical relation in a clause does not follow the verb of that clause, and that noun is not major third person singular, then a pronoun must take its place after the verb and be attached to the verb.[53] There are two kinds of third person pronouns which are necessarily attached to verbs: the non-DTP plural pronoun <u>aawa</u> and the three DTP pronouns listed below. The DTP pronouns require deletion of a preceding vowel in certain cases.

Distinct Third Person Pronouns

s	anim.p	inan.p
-áyi	-aiksi	-aistsi

Supplemental Material

There are what could be called non-affirmative pronouns as well. These will be discussed briefly in chapter 21. For now, we simply list them as <u>-atsiksi</u> '3s/in.s', <u>-aiksaawa</u> '3p/4p', and <u>-aistsaawa</u> 'ip'.

---

[53]There are examples in section 4.6.4 of chapter 20 in which DTP pronouns are attached to nominalized verbs.

CHAPTER TEN

Transitive Animate Part 1: Direct

A. INTRODUCTION

As explained in chapter 7, a TA verb agrees with its subject and with its animate gender object. The large number of person and number combinations of subject and object results in an extensive paradigm of forms, but most of these include affixes which we have already encountered above. In this chapter we look at a relatively straightforward portion of the TA paradigm, and build upon this in chapters 11 and 12. The entire TA paradigm is presented in chart form in Appendix A.

B. {1s,2s} SUBJECT with {3,4} OBJECT

Consider the following sentences:[54]

(a) *Nit*sikákomimma*wa* nitána.   "I love my daughter."
(b) *Nit*sikákomimma*yi* nitániksi.   "I love my daughters."
(c) *Kit*sikákomimma*wa* nitána.   "You$_{2s}$ love my daughter."
(d) *Kit*sikákomimma*yi* nitániksi.   "You$_{2s}$ love my daughters."
(e) *Nit*sikákomimma*yini* otáni.   "I love his daughter."
(f) *Nit*sikákomimma*yi* otániksi.   "I love his daughters."

Comparing (a)-(f) and noting the highlighted affixes, it seems there is nothing new to learn in this portion of the TA paradigm, for these same affixes are used in the AI and TI paradigms. But when these forms are compared to the remainder of the paradigm, especially in chapters 11 and 12, we will see that

---

[54]The verb stem for 'love', like many other verb stems in Blackfoot, seldom is used without the intensifier prefix <u>ik</u>; consequently, that prefix when used on such verbs is of virtually no semantic effect.

more is involved here than simply adding prefixes which agree with the subject and suffixes which agree with the object. In particular, we will see in section E that the stem for 'love' in these examples is ikakomimm, and the a which precedes the highlighted suffixes in (a)-(f) is a morpheme.

C. 1 AND 2 PLURAL AFFIXES

Consider (g) and (h):

(g) Nitsikákomimma*nnaan*i kitániksi.   "We$_{1p}$ love your daughters."
(h) Kitsikákomimma*waa*yi nitániksi.   "You$_{2p}$ love my daughters."

These sentences show that the TA verb uses suffixes to mark 1st and 2nd person plural which are nearly identical to affixes seen earlier (see section B of chapter 4). They differ in that the pluralizers here lack the hp, which appears on the 1p and 2p suffixes whenever they are used on a verb which does not also have a third person as subject or object. Other predictable variation in the verb pluralizer shape is as follows: The 1p suffix is innaan after a consonant, but usually just nnaan after a vowel. If nothing other than a clitic pronoun is attached, the 2p suffix is oaawa (see *e.g.* (b) of chapter 12), but is usually oaa otherwise (as in (h));[55] furthermore, when the 2p suffix is preceded by a vowel, the o is replaced by w according to a regular phonological rule, which also accounts for i and y alternations:[56]

Desyllabification

$\{i \rightarrow y, o \rightarrow w\} / V\_V$,   where the i and o do not carry accent

As was also seen in the TI paradigm of chapter 8, the pluralizers for first and second person precede suffixes for third person.

D. 21 AND UNSPECIFIED SUBJECT

The agreement affixes for 21 as subject do double duty, in that they are also used when the speaker does not wish to specify a subject. Observe the following:

---

[55]Forms in which -oaawa is followed by a suffix other than a pronoun are also relatively common, but as free variants of forms in which -oaa appears.

[56]There are apparent counterexamples to this rule as consequence of the convention which spells long vowels as a sequence of two like vowels. For example, áóoyiwa "he eats" appears to have an o between two vowels, but in its underlying form the first syllable of this word is a sequence of just two vowels: á and long oo.

(i) Ikákomimma*wa* kitána.   "We$_{21}$ love your daughter."
                             / "Your daughter is loved."
(j) Ikákomimma*yi* kitániksi. "We$_{21}$ love your daughters."
                             / "Your daughters are loved."
(k) Ikákomimma*yini* otáni. "We$_{21}$ love her daughter."
                             / "Her daughter is loved."

Notice that these 21/unspecified subject forms with third person object differ from the 1s and 2s subject forms (a)-(e) in lacking person prefixes.

E. 3 SUBJECT with 4 OBJECT

Recall that only one animate gender third person may be major third person (3); any others must be demoted to 4. (See section D of chapter 2.) So if both the subject and the object of a TA verb are third persons, one must be demoted. Here we will deal with the case in which the object is demoted; *i.e.* 3 subject with a 4 object. (4 subject with a 3 object will be dealt with in the next chapter.) This requires a new suffix in place of the a which follows the stem in (a)-(k).[57] It has two forms: -yii and -ii. -yii is used with stems which end in a vowel other than a, and -ii is used elsewhere. Examples follow:

(l) Ikákomimm*ii*wa nohkówa kitáni.   "My son loves your daughter."
(m) Isspómmo*yii*wa aakííkoana póósi. "The girl helped the cat."
(n) Iisína*ii*wa nínaawa pookááyi.
    "The man took a picture of the child."

Such TA forms show number agreement with their subjects but not with their objects. Compare (o) and (p) with (l). Notice that pluralizing the subject 'son' affects the verb inflection, but pluralizing the object 'daughter' does not:

(o) Ikákomimmiiyi nohkóíksi kitáni. "My sons love your daughter."
(p) Ikákomimmiiwa nohkówa kitániksi. "My son loves your daughters."

The same suffix -yii ~ -ii is used when a minor third person is subject and another minor third person[58] is object. In such cases as well, the verbs show number agreement with their subjects but not with their objects. Compare (q) with (r) and (s):

---

[57]In the next chapter we will refer to these suffixes as 'direct (dir) theme' suffixes.

[58]Indicated as a 5 in paradigm 3. of Appendix A.

(q) Iisínaiiyini anna nínaawa ohkóyi pookááyi.
   iisína-ii-yini ann-wa nínaa-wa w-ohkó-yi pookáá-yi
   picture(TA)-dir-4s that-3s man-3s 3-son-4s child-4s
   "The man's son took a picture of the child."

(r) Iisínaiiyi anna nínaawa ohkóíksi pookááyi.
   iisína-ii-yi ann-wa nínaa-wa w-ohkó-iksi pookáá-yi
   picture(TA)-dir-4p that-3s man-3s 3-son-4p child-4s
   "The man's sons took a picture of the child."

(s) Iisínaiiyini anna nínaawa ohkóyi pookáíksi.
   iisína-ii-yini ann-wa nínaa-wa w-ohkó-yi pookáá-iksi
   past:picture(TA)-dir-4s that-3s man-3s 3-son-4s child-4p
   "The man's son took a picture of the children."

EXERCISE

Add the correct TA agreement affixes to the verbs of the following sentences. (The verb is the first word in each example.) Be sure to add a theme suffix (either <u>a</u> or <u>ii</u>~<u>yii</u>), as seen in (a)-(p), to the stems given below before adding the agreement affixes. [Alternatively, consult paradigm 3 of Appendix A for the correct theme suffix and agreement affixes.]

1. áisspommo   nohkóíksi
    "You$_{2s}$ help my sons."

2. yiimat   anna aakííkoana ónni
    "We$_{1p}$ imitated the girl's father."

3. itsit   saahkómaapiwa
    "I caught up to the boy."

4. ohpopaat   i'naksípokaiksi
    "You$_{2p}$ held the babies on your laps."

5. inakat   pokóna
    "We$_{21}$ rolled the ball/ the ball was rolled."

6. áakohtookisat   aakííkoana ohsíssi.
    "The girl will ask her younger sibling to translate (for her)."

7. innissko   pookáíksi imitáíksi
    "The kids chased off the dogs".

CHAPTER ELEVEN

Transitive Animate Part 2: Inverse

A. DIRECT VS. INVERSE THEME

In the previous chapter we saw examples such as (a) and (b):

(a) Nitsikákomimmawa nitána.   "I love my daughter."
(b) Nitsikákomimmayi nitániksi.   "I love my daughters."

Now compare the following examples; note the highlighted portion:

(c) Nitsikákomimm*ok*a nitána.   "My daughter loves me."
(d) Nitsikákomimm*ok*i nitániksi.   "My daughters love me."

Given that the verbs of (c) and (d) end in suffixes <u>wa</u> and <u>yi</u> (with the semivowels lost after a consonant), these sentences differ from their (a) and (b) counterparts only in that the verb stems of (c) and (d) end in <u>ok</u> while the verb stems of (a) and (b) end in <u>a</u>. The portion of verb stems under discussion is referred to as the **theme** suffix. The suffix <u>a</u> of (a) and (b) is known as the **direct** theme suffix (dir), and the suffix <u>ok</u> of (c) and (d) as the **inverse** theme suffix (inv). Verbs with first or second person subject and third person object are direct, while those with third person subject and first or second person object are inverse. The <u>ii</u>~<u>yii</u> suffix added to stems with 3 as subject and 4 as object (seen in preceding chapter) can also be considered a direct theme suffix.[59]

Here are some more sentences containing inverse forms; note that they utilize the same suffixes for person and number that we saw on the direct verb forms in the previous chapter:

(e) **Kit**sikákomimm*oka* nitána.   "My daughter loves you$_{2s}$."

---

[59] Although its use in a type of nominalization (see section 5.2 of chapter 20) suggests it might be an intransitivizing suffix.

(f) *Kit*sikákomimmok*i* nitániksi.   "My daughters love you$_{2s}$."
(g) *Nit*sikákomimmok*ini* otáni.   "His daughter loves me."
(h) *Nit*sikákomimmok*i* otániksi.   "His daughters love me."
(i) *Nit*sikákomimmok*innaan*i kitániksi.   "Your daughters love us$_{1p}$."
(j) *Kit*sikákomimmok*oaa*yi kitániksi.   "Your daughters love you$_{2p}$."

B. 4 SUBJECT with 3 OBJECT

Verbs with minor third person subject and major third person object are inverse as well:

(k) *Ot*sikákomimmok*a* nohkówa otáni.   "Her daughter loves my son."
(l) *Ot*sikákomimmok*oaayi* nohkóíksi otáni.   "Her daughter loves my sons."
(m) *Ot*sikákomimmok*a* nohkówa otániksi.   "Her daughters love my son."

There are two important things to notice about verbs with this combination of subject and object. First, these are the only verb forms in any *independent* paradigm which have a prefix that indicates third person, and in which oaa(wa)yi rather than just yi marks '3p'. Second, although the prefix ot and the inverse theme suffix are found together only with the 4→3 person combination, these forms have no affixes which agree with the minor third person. They agree only with the major third person; note that number of 'daughter' is not reflected in the verbs of (k)-(m).

C. SUMMARY OF TA AFFIX POSITIONS

In addition to the theme suffix just discussed, and which we will consider to be part of the stem of TA verbs, there are three agreement affix positions, which we will refer to as AGR1, AGR2, and AGR3. AGR1 is a prefix and the other two are suffixes, with AGR2 preceding AGR3 if both are present. These facts can be summarized in the following "formula" for the TA verb (TAV):

TAV = AGR1 + STEM + AGR2 + AGR3

Here are lists of the AGR affixes arranged in columns under their respective positions of occurrence:[60]

---

[60]See section C of chapter 10 regarding the parenthesized portions of these affixes.

Transitive Animate Inverse

	AGR1		AGR2		AGR3
kit-	'2'	-(i)nnaan	'1p'	-wa	'3s'
nit-	'1'	-oaa(wa)	'2p'	-yi	'3p/4p'
ot-	'3'	-oaa(wa)	'3p'	-yini	'4s'

No one of the AGR positions must be filled in all TA verbs, but no TA independent verbs occur without at least one of them containing an affix. Also, only one of the affixes in a column may occur in any given verb. As we shall see, there are precedence relations within each set, in the sense that if agreement generalizations call for more than one affix from a given set, the actually occurring affix is determined by rule. In the chart above, the affixes in each set are arranged so that an affix takes precedence over those below it in the same set.

D. VARIANT SHAPES OF THE INVERSE SUFFIX

In all of the examples above, the inverse theme suffix has the shape <u>ok</u>. However it also takes two other forms in independent verbs, depending upon the preceding segment. If the preceding segment is a <u>t</u>, then this <u>t</u> plus the inverse suffix are together realized as a long <u>kk</u>,[61] as illustrated in (n); compare the direct form (o):

(n) Nitsínaka*kk*a.   "He rolled me."
(o) Nitsínakatawa.   "I rolled him."

If the preceding segment is an <u>i</u>, the inverse suffix is <u>ook</u>, as seen in (p):

(p) Nitáwayáki*ook*a.   "He hit me."

This latter form of the inverse suffix is called for even if the preceding <u>i</u> is deleted by i-Absorption, as it is in (q), or by i-Loss, as it is in (r):[62]

(q) Nitókskoihts*ook*a.   "He covered me (with a blanket)."
    nit-okskoihtsi-ook-wa
    1-cover(TA)-inv-3s

(r) Nitsíípohkisstoy*ook*a. "He shaved me."
    nit-IIpohkisstoyi-ook-wa
    1-pst:shave(TA)-inv-3s

---

[61] This gemmination is included as phonological rule 1 in Appendix B.

[62] So the <u>o</u> of this suffix is one of the variable-length vowels to be discussed in chapter 15, and can be represented as <u>o:</u>.

Elsewhere the inverse suffix has the form ok.[63]

EXERCISE

Add the correct TA agreement affixes to the verbs of the following sentences. (The verb is the first word in each example.) Be sure to add the correct theme suffix to the verb stems provided. [Alternatively, consult paradigm 3 of Appendix A for the correct theme suffix and agreement affixes.]

1. áísspommo   nohkóíksi   "My sons help you$_{2s}$."

2. yiimat   anna aakííkoana ónni   "The girl's father imitated me."

3. itsit   saahkómaapiwa   "The boy caught up to me."

4. aawayáki   nisskána omiksi saahkómaapiiksi
"Those boys hit my younger sibling." (Notice that nisskána 'my younger sibling' is marked as major third person.)

5. iipohkisstoyi   nitákkaawa   "My friend shaved me."

6. áakohtookisat   aakííkoana ohsíssi.
"Her younger sibling$_{4s}$ will ask the girl$_{3s}$ to translate (for her)."

---

[63]There are at least two other morphemes which have variants involving o: ~ ∅. When such morphemes appear in paradigm charts in the appendix, they are represented as beginning with O.

CHAPTER TWELVE

Transitive Animate Part 3

A. 1ST PERSON SUBJECT WITH 2ND PERSON OBJECT

So far, all of the TA forms we have discussed involved third person as either subject or object. In this chapter we look at TA forms which do not involve an overt third person as either subject or object.

(a) *Kit*sikákomimm*o*. "I love you$_{2s}$."
(b) *Kit*sikákomimm*ohpoaawa*. "I love you$_{2p}$."

In chapters 10 and 11 we saw that if first or second person is subject or object, the verb prefix reflects that fact. But the verbs we are considering in this and the next section have both first and second person involved, one as subject and the other as object. At the end of chapter 11 we listed three agreement affix positions for TA verbs and said that only one affix could be in each position at a time. So if rules call for more than one, there must be a precedence rule that determines which has priority. We see in (a) and (b) that second person "wins out" over first person in that the AGR1 prefix[64] is <u>kit</u>, which we have seen to agree with second person. Following the stem <u>ikakomimm</u> in (a) is a theme suffix <u>o</u> which serves the dual purpose of indicating that first person is involved and that first person is subject; the latter function of the suffix will be more evident when further forms are presented in the next section. Comparing (b) we see that the same second person pluralizer seen in AI verbs is in the AGR2 position. Next we pluralize first person to get (c):[65]

(c) *Kit*sikákomimm*ohpinnaan*a. "We love you$_{2s/2p}$."

---

[64]See section C of chapter 11.

[65]The final <u>a</u> in (c), like the final <u>a</u> mentioned in footnote 17 of chapter 4, is present only to prevent a word from ending in a consonant.

As the reader might have expected, the same 1p suffix seen in AI verbs is in the AGR2 position. But notice that the English translation indicates that this form will also be used if both first and second person are plural. This shows us that 1p has priority over 2p where the AGR2 position is concerned; the presence of the 1p suffix makes it impossible to indicate 2p. That is, the obligatory absence of a 2p suffix in (c) precludes any indication of the number of second person.

The o of the 1 → 2 forms is long after stems which end in i̱; so it too is one of the variable-length vowels to be discussed in chapter 15. In the charts of Appendix A this vowel is represented by o:.

B. 2ND PERSON SUBJECT WITH 1ST PERSON OBJECT

(d) Kitsikákomimm*oki*.   "You$_{2s}$ love me."
(e) Kitsikákomimm*oki*hpoaawa.   "You$_{2p}$ love me."
(f) Kitsikákomimm*oki*hpinnaana. "You$_{2s/2p}$ love us$_{1p}$."

Comparing these forms to those in section A, we observe that these have -oki where (a)-(c) have -o. The ok portion is evidently the inverse theme suffix introduced in chapter 11;[66] the remaining i̱ serves to indicate that the other person involved is 1st person.

The presence of the inverse theme suffix in (d)-(f) can be accounted for by concluding that in the Blackfoot agreement system, 1st person outranks 2nd person. The -o of the 1→2 forms in (a)-(c) must then be seen to simultaneously serve as a direct theme suffix and as indicator of 1st person involvement, as stated in section A. Discussion of the plural suffixes of (a)-(c) applies without change to (d)-(f).

C. UNSPECIFIED SUBJECT WITH 1ST OR 2ND PERSON OBJECT

(g) Kitsikákomimm*okoo*(wa).   "You$_{2s}$ are loved."
(h) Nitsikákomimm*okoo*(wa).   "I am loved."

Sentences (g) and (h) have TA forms which are used when the subject (the "lover" in this case) is unspecified (but assumed to be "mind-possessing"). They involve the inverse theme suffix plus an additional oo. As problematic as

---

[66]It has exactly the same variant shapes in the same environments described in chapter 11.

this oo is for analysis, the situation is even more complex, as we see when we add the plural forms in (i)-(k):

(i) Kitsikákomimm*ot*sspoaawa.   "You$_{2p}$ are loved."
(j) Nitsikákomimm*ot*sspinnaan(a).   "We$_{1p}$ are loved."
(k) Ikákomimm*ot*sspa.   "We$_{21}$ are loved."

In (i) and (j) we see the 1p and 2p suffixes hpinnaan and hpoaawa, as we might expect, but in place of the inverse theme suffix ok and the suffix oo, we find -ot+i. (Postsibilation accounts for the ss; see chapter 5.) And the marking of 21 by -hpa in (k) is unique in the TA independent paradigm.

Like the o of the inverse suffix -ok, the o of -ot is null after stems which end in t, as in (l); otherwise it is realized as o: (see chapter 15, section B, regarding variable length vowels such as o:), as seen in (m) (compare (i)).

(l) Áyiimattsspa.   "We$_{21}$ are being imitated."
   á-yiimat-tsi-hpa
   dur-imitate(TA)-inverse-21

(m) Kitáakai'stamattsootsspoaawa.   "You$_{2p}$ will be instructed."
   kit-yáak-wai'stamattsi-o:tsi-hpoaawa
   2-fut-instruct(TA)-inverse-2p

D. TA WITH INANIMATE LOGICAL SUBJECT

As explained in section C of chapter 8, Blackfoot transitive verbs must have subjects which are capable of exercising a will.[67] So if the logical subject of a TA verb does not meet that requirement, the following strategy is followed: an unspecified subject form of the TA verb is used (see preceding section and section D of chapter 10), and the involvement of the logical subject is indicated by use of the "linking" prefix iiht~oht~omoht 'means' (see section 4 of chapter 16). This has the consequence that such sentences are ambiguous, for they are then open to an interpretation in which an unspecified animate subject is involved and the intended inanimate logical subject is simply a means or instrument and not the logical subject at all. Note the two meanings given for the following example:

---

[67]Some speakers allow a non-volitional stimulus as subject of a TA verb with an experiencer as object: Nítsskíi'tsooka ómi ataksáaksini. 'That box frightened me.' (From Greg Thomson, personal communication.)

(n) Amo isttoána nomohtsipohkisstoyookoo(wa).
  amo isttoáN-wa n-omoht-Ipohkisstoyi-ook-oo
  this knife-3s 1-means-shave(TA)-inv-unspec
  "This knife shaved me."/ "I was shaved with this knife."

If the object of such a verb is third person, the unspecified subject form (section D of chapter 10) is the same as the TA form with 21 as subject, so the resultant sentence is three ways ambiguous:

(o) Anni miistísi iihtawayákiaawa imitááwa.
  ann-yi miistsíS-yi iiht-wa:wayáki-a:-wa imitááw-wa
  that-in.s stick-in.s means-hit(TA)-dir-3s dog-3s
  "That stick hit the dog."/"The dog was hit with a stick."
  / "We$_{21}$ hit the dog with a stick."

EXERCISE

Translate the following into Blackfoot:
(Note: All necessary verb stems may be found in chapters 10, 11, and 12.)

1. I have helped you$_{2p}$.

2. I will shave you$_{2s}$.

3. You$_{2s}$ are imitating me.

4. We$_{1p}$ were photographed. (verb stem is <u>sina</u>)

5. We$_{21}$ will be instructed.

6. I was covered (with a blanket).

7. That knife shaved you$_{2p}$.

CHAPTER THIRTEEN

Demonstratives

There are five demonstrative stems to which numerous suffixes may be added.[68] In this chapter we will deal primarily with the basic stems and their inflectional forms.

A. THE BASIC STEMS

Each demonstrative stem carries information regarding proximity of its referent to the speaker, as well as proximity or presumed familiarity of its referent to the addressee. Here are the basic stems and an indication of the proximity information they carry:

amo proximity to speaker but not to addressee
om proximity to neither speaker nor addressee
anno proximity to the speaker
       and proximity or familiarity to the addressee
ann proximity or familiarity to the addressee
       but no proximity to the speaker
am proximity and familiarity to the speaker

Corresponding to each of the five stems given above are what Taylor (1978) calls "diminutives"; these are, respectively, amssto, omsst, annssto, annsst, and amsst.[69] They are used for referents which the speaker views with pathos or affection: generally old persons and children.

---

[68]There are verb stems which are derived from demonstrative stems, but we will not deal with those here.

[69]The position of an apparent diminutive suffix sst in these stems supports Taylor's analysis of demonstratives amo and anno as including a suffix o. However, because of difficulty in assigning a consistent meaning or function to the latter suffix, I am of the opinion that the present under-analysis is more practical for the intended audience of these chapters.

B. USES

Demonstratives may be used alone as free pronouns as in (a)-(d), or as modifiers of nouns as in (e)-(j). In either case they take the same inflectional suffixes (highlighted in (a)-(d)) seen on nouns in earlier chapters, except that after amo and anno there are two irregularities: the animate singular suffix is null (as in (g)), and the initial i of suffixes such as -iksi and -istsi is lost (as in (b)), though occasionally the initial i of -istsi may be heard after these stems, as in (e) and (j).

(a) Amo*yi* nítohpommatoo'pa.   "I bought this (inan)."
    amo-yi nit-ohpommatoo-'p-wa
    this-in.s 1-buy(TI)-theme-in.s

(b) Áaksowatayi ámo*ksi*.   "We₂₁ will eat these (anim)."
    yáak-Iowat-aa-yi amo-ksi
    fut-eat(TA)-dir-3p this-3p

(c) Nohkówa nítohkokka ann*i*.   "My son gave me that (inan or 4)."
    n-ohkó-wa nit-ohkot-k-wa ann-yi
    1-son-3s 1-give(TA)-inv-3s that-in.s/4s

(d) Om*istsi* íikssoka'piiyaawa.   "Those (inan) are good."
    om-istsi iik-soka'pii-yi-aawa
    that-ip very-good(II)-ip-PRO

Of course when demonstratives modify nouns their inflectional suffixes must agree with those of the modified noun, as in (e)-(j). For example, in (e) both the demonstrative glossed 'this' and the noun for 'berry' have the inanimate plural ('ip') suffix istsi:

(e) Amo(i)stsi míínistsi iikááhsiiyaawa.   "These berries are good."
    amo-istsi míín-istsi iik-aahsii-yi-aawa
    this-ip berry-ip very-good-ip-PRO

(f) Nítsskiitatoo'pi annistsi mí'kskapayinistsi.   "I baked those crackers."
    nit-ihkiitatoo-'p-yi ann-istsi mí'ksk-apayin-istsi
    1-bake(TI)-theme-ip that-ip hard-bread-ip

(g) Amo ní'sa ikákomimmiiwa anni kissísi.
    amo n-i's-wa ikakomimm-yii-wa ann-yi k-iihsís-yi
    this 1-ol.bro-3s love-dir-3s that-4s 2-yo.sibl-4s
    "My brother loves your little sister."

Demonstratives

(h) Anni otánoaawayi áóoyo'siyináyi.   "Their daughter cooks."
    ann-yi w-itán-oaawa-yi á-ooyo'si-yini-áyi
    that-4s 3-daughter-3p-4s dur-cook-4s-PRO

(i) Annáhka Sámahka áako'toowa.   "Sam will arrive."
    ann-wa-hka Sam-wa-hka yáak-o'too-wa
    that-3s-invs Sam-3s-invs fut-arrive-3s

(j) Annó(í)stsi miistákistsi, nitsítokooyi.
    anno-istsi miistak-istsi nit-it-okooyi
    this-ip mountain-ip 1-there-dwell
    "Here in these mountains, I live."

As can be observed in (g)-(i), Blackfoot, unlike English, often uses demonstratives to modify kin terms and proper nouns.[70]

C. ACCENT ON DEMONSTRATIVES

Either syllable of a demonstrative may be accented, depending upon factors which are not as yet fully understood by this investigator. However, these factors do seem to include the following:

1. Whether or not the demonstrative is being used in the first mention of its referent in the current discourse.

2. With amo, om, ann, and am, accent on the first syllable may emphasize the proximity features which distinguish these basic stems. *E.g*, a speaker may accent the first syllable of ómiksi in order to emphasize the lack of proximity to the speaker and addressee of its referents. (Taylor 1978)

D. ACCENT AND LENGTH

Although accent and length are independent features of vowels elsewhere in the language, in the demonstrative stems the accented vowel is always lengthened, except before the long consonant of ann and anno. However, because this length is automatic in demonstratives, it has not beeen indicated in their spelling here. (Of course, indication of such length is not incorrect.)

E. SOME POST-INFLECTIONAL SUFFIXES

There are at least four suffixes which may be attached to inflected demonstratives (and accompanying nouns). The four are listed here with their central meanings (and abbreviations for later glosses):[71]

---

[70] 'invs' abbreviates 'invisible'. See section E. below regarding the suffix so glossed.

[71] The meanings for all but the last are from Taylor (1978).

-ma	"stationary" (stat)
-ya	"moving, but not toward speaker" (movg)[72]
-hka	"not visible to the speaker" (invs)[73]
-ka	"proximity information in the demonstrative is relative to location of the speaker or addressee at a time other than the time of the speech act" (o.t.)

Examples follow:

(k) Amoma miistsísa áakitohkitopiiyináyi.
    amo-ma miistsíS-wa yáak-it-ohkit-opii-yini-áyi
    this-stat tree-3s fut-there-upon-sit-4s-PRO
"He will sit on this tree."

(l) Amoya áyo'kaawa iipánna'poowa.
    amo-ya á-yo'kaa-wa iipann-a'p-oo-wa
    this-movg dur-sleep-3s overnight-about-go-3s
"This sleeping one was going about all night."

(m) Anná annáhka kínnahka?
    ann-wa ann-wa-hka k-ínn-wa-hka
    where-3s that-3s-invs 2-father-3s-invs
"Where is your father?"

(n) Áó'tahkayiiniki, amíka nookóówayika
    a'-o'tahkayi-iniki am-yi-ka n-ookóówa-yi-ka
    when-arrv.hm-1s(subj)[74] this-in.s-o.t. 1-home-in.s-o.t.

        nitáaka'páísoksistotsii'pa.
        nit-yáak-a'p-á-sok-Istotsi-'p-wa
        1-fut-PREF-dur-well-build(TI)-theme-3s

"When I get home, I'll fix my house up."

---

[72]This gloss is in need of revision. Current research seems to indicate that if motion is involved in the meaning of this suffix, it is not necessarily taking place at the time of the speech act, as example (k) shows, or even at the time of the process, event, or state being described.

[73]According to Greg Thomson (personal communication) the apparent use of this suffix to mark words referring to entities which are not visible is a consequence of the discourse function of this suffix, which has to do with saliency.

[74]'subj' abbreviates Subjunctive; see chapter 19.

(o) ámoksika isttsííksinai'kokaiksika
    amo-ksi-ka isttsííksina-i'kokaa-iksi-ka
    this-3p-o.t. snake-paint^lodge-3p-o.t.[75]
    "ones who (used) snake-painted lodges here"

In certain cases demonstratives with these suffixes have a specialized use or meaning. In particular, note the following:

annóma "around here"   annohka "now"
annama "the late (*i.e.* deceased) ..."

F. POSITION OF DEMONSTRATIVES AS MODIFIERS

Demonstratives always precede the nouns which they modify (their **Head**s), as seen above in (e)-(j). The only thing which can separate a demonstrative from its Head is a nominalized verb[76] which also modifies the same Head. Examples are (p) and (q):

(p) oma áyo'kaawa nínaawa   "that sleeping man"
                            / "that man who is sleeping"
(q) omiksi áínihkiiksi aakííkoaksi "those singing girls"

EXERCISES

1. Given: <u>amo</u> <u>ponokáómitaawa</u> 'this horse (near speaker)'
   Translate: 'those horses (near addressee)'

2. Given: <u>omistsi</u> <u>míínistsi</u> 'those berries (not near addressee)'
   Translate: 'this berry (near speaker)'

3. Given: example (a) of section B above
   Translate: 'I bought those (near addressee).'

4. Given: example (c) above
   Translate: 'My sons gave me these (near speaker and addressee).'

---

[75] The symbol '^' is used to connect multiword glosses of single Blackfoot morphemes.

[76] The examples provided here will be intransitive verb stems inflected as nouns; such nouns always reference the underlying subject of the verb. Nominalization processes will be discussed in chapter 20.

5. Given: examples (g) and (h) above
   Translate: 'Those (near addressee) my brothers are cooking.'

CHAPTER FOURTEEN

Possessives

Possessed nouns are marked for person and number of their possessors, by affixes which we will call **possessive affixes**. In addition, and following any possessive suffixes, are the usual inflectional suffixes expected on nouns and summarized in section E of chapter 2. Below are some examples, with the possessive affixes highlighted; observe that they are much like the agreement affixes seen on verbs in earlier chapters; the major differences are that "inclusive our" (21) is marked by a combination of the second person prefix (kit ~ k) and a new suffix (i)nnoon,[77] a third person possessor calls for a new prefix ot ~ w, and the third person plural possessive suffix is oaawa. (The full paradigm of possessive affixes will be presented in section E.)

(a) amo aakííkoana *o*ksísstsi   "this girl's mother"
(b) *n*iksíssta   "my mother"
(c) *n*iksísst*sinnaan*a   "our$_{1p}$ mother"
(d) *k*iksísst*sinnoon*iksi   "our$_{21}$ mothers"
(e) *k*itákkaa*nnoon*a   "our$_{21}$ friend"
(f) anna nínaawa *ot*ohkáksaakini   "the man's axe"
(g) anniksi pookáíksi o'ts*óaawa*istsi "the children's hands"
(h) *nit*ómitaamiksi   "my dogs"

In (a) the highlighted o actually represents two segments: a prefix w plus the initial vowel i of the stem. These are realized as o as a result of the following new phonological rule:

---

[77]The initial i of this suffix is present after consonants and o. Some speakers replace it by o after consonants.

Coalescence

$$w + i(\colon) \to o$$

The i in the rule may be either long or short, as the notation i(:) is intended to indicate.

In (g), no prefix is highlighted. This is because the prefix here again is w, and a glide cannot remain at the beginning of words in Blackfoot. This is accounted for by the following rule:

Semivowel Drop

$$G \to \emptyset\ /\ \#\_\ ,\ \ \ \text{where '\#' indicates a word boundary}^{78}$$

Example (g) also demonstrates that Desyllabification (of the o in oaawa) is prevented from applying (*i.e.* is bled) by i-Absorption, rather than vice versa, or else the form would be *o'tsíwaawaistsi from w+o'tsi+oaawa+istsi.[79]

There are various properties of nouns with regard to possession which can be used to classify them, including whether possessive inflection is obligatory (*i.e.* whether the noun never occurs without possessive inflection), whether the noun requires a suffix (i)m before possessive affixes may be added, and in the case of simple noun stems, whether it selects the short or long person prefixes.[80] We will divide nouns into three classes with regard to optionality/necessity of possessive inflection. These are presented in sections A - C.

A. OPTIONALLY POSSESSED STEMS

Examples (f) and (g) above illustrate stems which are optionally possessed; compare the following examples of the same stems without possessive inflection:

(i) káksaakina   "axe"
(j) mo'tsísi   "hand"

As usual, the first morpheme of the stem determines whether the short or long

---

[78]Obviously, this rule does not bleed the rule Coalescence, which was introduced just above.

[79]Actually, there is indeterminacy here, for the sequence Ciwa is often (in certain positions) pronounced [Co(w)a] anyway. If this process, i → o / C_w{a,o} , call it Coalescence 2, is a phonological rule rather than a fast speech phenomenon, (g) might arise by Desyllabification followed by Coalescence 2.

[80]Another property which most analysts utilize in classification is whether the noun has an (apparent) m prefix when no other person prefix is present. See section D.

person prefixes are used. As can be seen in (f) and (g), ohkáksaakin 'axe'[81] selects the long prefixes and mo'tsíS 'hand' selects the short prefixes. Here are additonal examples of optionally possessed nouns which select the long prefixes:

(k) otsístotoohsiists   "her clothes"
(l) nitsísttokimaa'tsisi   "my drum"

B. OBLIGATORILY POSSESSED STEMS

(a) - (e) above are examples of obligatorily possessed stems; these are nouns which never occur without the possessive affixes.[82] They are inherently relational in that they necessarily reference two parties: one is the **primary referent** of the noun stem itself, and the other, which we will call the **relatee**, is the party or parties to which the primary referent bears the expressed relation. For example, the stem inn 'father' expresses a relation between two parties; consequently, it requires reference to the one **who is** father as primary referent, and to the one or more relatee(s) (*i.e.* his offspring) **to whom** the primary referent is father. Here are some other relational stems, with indication of primary referent and relatee:

rel. stem	gloss	primary referent	relatee
iksisst	mother	one who is mother	offspring
ohko	son	one who is son	parent
itan	daughter	one who is daughter	parent
i's	older brother	one who is older brother	sibling (younger)
ookoowa	home	dwelling	dweller

For such relational nouns, the possessive affixes reference the relatee. Here are examples used in sentences:

(m) Kiksísstsinnooniksi áyo'kaayaawa.   "Our$_{21}$ mothers are sleeping."
(n) Amo aakííkoana oksísstsi áyo'kaayináyi.
    "This girl's mother is sleeping."
(o) Nomohtó'too anná nínaawa ookóówayi. "I came from the man's house."

Most such stems use the short form of the person agreement prefixes (unless some other morpheme which calls for the long form is first prefixed to the stem).

---

[81] See the next chapter regarding the oh of 'axe'.
[82] Such stems are sometimes called "inalienably possessed".

C. DERIVED RELATIONAL STEMS

Example (h) is an obligatorily possessed stem derived from a noun stem which otherwise cannot take the possessive affixes. Such relational nouns are formed by addition of -(i)m (glossed 'poss' in examples below). This suffix has slightly different realizations with different stems, and the actual form it takes does not seem to be completely predictable. It generally has the form -im if the stem to which the suffix is added ends in a consonant: nitóóhkotokimi 'my rock'; but with certain consonant final stems, the i is inexplicably long: nitohpóósiima 'my cat'.[83] When added to a stem which ends in a short vowel, the suffix either has the form -im, as seen in nitsisttsiksípokoimi[84] 'my salt', or the stem-final vowel is lengthened and the suffix is -m, as in nitápotskinaama 'my cow'. When added to a stem which ends in a long vowel, the suffix is simply -m.[85]

These stems utilize the possessive affixes, which agree with the relatee as in section B above, but in general they use the long form of the person agreement prefixes (unless some other morpheme which calls for the short form is first prefixed to the stem). Here are more examples:[86]

(p) Nitómitaama áóhkiwa.   "My dog is barking."
    nit-omitaa-m-wa á-ohki-wa
    1-dog-poss-3s dur-bark-3s

(q) Kitápotskinaamoaawaiksi áóhkomiiyaawa.
    kit-ápotskina-:m-oaawa-iksi á-ohkomii-yi-aawa
    2-cow-poss-2p-3p   dur-call-3p-PRO
    "Your₂ₚ cows are mooing."

D. INITIAL NASAL LOSS

As will be seen in chapter 15, one of the most common variations in the shape of morphemes is the loss of an initial nasal when preceded by another morpheme in the same word; in fact, there are relatively few morphemes in Blackfoot which retain an initial nasal when not in word-initial position. So when most stems which begin with nasal-initial morphemes take possessive prefixes, the nasal is dropped: compare niistsíípisskaani 'fence' and

---

[83]The oh at the beginning of the stem for 'cat' is part of the non-initial variant of this stem; see chapter 15.

[84]There is considerable inter-speaker or dialectal variation here.

[85]One apparent exception is seen in nitsínaima 'my boss'. However, as stated on page 108, the stem Inaa 'leader/chief' has an allomorph with a short a when followed by a derivational suffix.

[86]The form of 'dog' seen in (h) has the non-initial variant of this stem; see chapter 15.

kitsistsíípisskaani 'your fence'. In the first form there is an initial n which is part of the stem, but in the second form with possessive prefix kit[87] the stem lacks this n. (The first vowel of the stem of 'fence' is long only when it is in the first syllable of a word; see chapter 15 for a brief discussion of such vowel length variation.) Here is an example with initial m: *mí*'sohpsskiiwa 'muskrat', nitsí'sohpsskiima 'my muskrat'.

Almost all Blackfoot stems for body parts have an initial m. As just described, that m will be present only if no prefix precedes these stems. This gives rise to paradigms such as the following:[88]

(r) móókoani "stomach"   (s) mo'tsísi "hand"
     nóókoani "my stomach"   no'tsísi "my hand"
     kóókoani "your stomach"   ko'tsísi "your hand"
     óókoani   "his stomach"   o'tsísi   "his hand"

Such paradigms give the initial m the appearance of a prefix, which has led most analysts to consider it a marker of unspecified possessor (often called "indefinite" possessor).[89] However, any prefix, not just a person prefix, eliminates the initial m, as seen in (t). This, plus the fact that several nouns which are not obligatorily possessed have an initial m only if no prefix precedes the stem (see the stem for 'muskrat' in the preceding paragraph for an example), favors the analysis presented here.

(t) i'náko'tsisi "small hand", kitsi'náko'tsisi "your small hand"

---

[87]Of course the t of kit- becomes ts before i by t-Affrication - see chapter 5.

[88]Observe that the 3rd person prefix w, in the words for 'his stomach' and 'his hand', results in absence of the m even though the w itself is eliminated by Semivowel Drop.

[89]See Frantz and Creighton 1982 for discussion and references.

E. THE POSSESSIVE AFFIX PARADIGM

person of "possessor"	number of "possessor"	
	sg	pl
1	n-/nit-...	n-/nit-...-(i)nnaan[90]
21	--------	k-/kit-...-(i)nnoon
2	k-/kit-...	k-/kit...-oaawa
3	w-/ot-...	w-/ot-...-oaawa
4	w-/ot-...(wa)	w-/ot-...-oaawa

The third person prefix w- is replaced by m- before stems beginning in a, as illustrated in (u):

(u) Anni *m*aaáhsi ákao'tooyináyi.   "His elder relation has arrived"
    ann-yi m-aaáhs-yi ákaa-o'too-yini-áyi
    that-4s 3-eld.relat-4s perf-arrive-4s-PRO

In addition to the possessive affixes, the possessed noun will carry the appropriate suffixes for its own gender, person (3 or 4), and number. (Remember that any animate gender noun possessed by 3 or 4 is necessarily 4.)

Here are full possessive paradigms for itán 'daughter' and ookóówa 'dwelling':

nitána	"my daughter"	nitáninnaana	"our$_{1p}$ daughter"
		kitáninnoona	"our$_{21}$ daughter"
kitána	"your$_{2s}$ daughter"	kitánoaawa(wa)	"your$_{2p}$ daughter"
otáni	"his$_3$ daughter"	otánoaawayi	"their daughter"
otánayi	"his$_4$ daughter"	otánoaawayi	"their daughter"

(*cf.* "daughters": nitániksi "my daughters"; nitáninnaaniksi "our daughters")

---

[90]The (i) of (i)nnaan and (i)nnoon is not present after stems ending in i, a, w, or y.

Possessives

nookóówayi	"my home"	nookóówannaani	"our$_{1p}$ home"
		kookóówannooni	"our$_{21}$ home"
kookóówayi	"your$_{2s}$ home"	kookóówawaawayi	"your$_{2p}$ home"
ookóówayi	"his$_3$ home"	ookóówawaawayi	"their home"
ookóówa(wa)yi	"his$_4$ home"	ookóówawaawayi	"their home"

(*cf.* "homes": ookóówaistsi "his homes"; kookóówannoonistsi "our$_{21}$ homes")

F. NOUNS AS POSSESSORS

A noun as possessor is positioned before the noun which it modifies, as seen in (u):

(u) oma nínaawa ohkóyi   "that man's son"

If the possessed noun is also modified by a demonstrative,[91] that demonstrative will follow the noun as possessor; note the position of <u>omiksi</u> in (v):

(v) amo nínna omiksi óta'siksi   "my father's horses"

The demonstrative <u>omiksi</u> 'those' modifies <u>óta'siksi</u> 'his horses', while <u>amo</u> 'this' modifies <u>nínna</u> 'my father'.

G. THE INDEPENDENT PRONOUN PARADIGM

The independent pronouns mentioned in section A of chapter 4 are possessed forms of an animate gender stem <u>iistó</u>. They are presented here, utilizing the same person and number abbreviations as were used in the earlier possessive paradigms.

---

[91] See chapter 13 on demonstratives.

person of "possessor"	number of "possessor"	
	sg	pl
1	niistówa	niistónnaana
21	--------	kiistónnoona
2	kiistówa	kiistówaawa
3	ostóyi	ostówaawayi

Notice that these pronouns seem to have the '3s' suffix wa and the '4s' suffix yi as would any animate gender noun. Even the non-third person pronouns will have the wa suffix replaced by a yi suffix when they are used in clauses involving another animate gender noun, unless the pronoun functions as subject. Observe the following examples:

(w) Niistóyi, nitsinóóka annáhka nohkówahka.
   "My son saw *me*."
(x) Oma nitákkaawa nómohtsistsinikooka kiistóyi.
   "My friend told me about you."
(y) Anniksi pookáíksi iihtsspíyiyaawa niistónnaani.
   "The children danced for us."

In (w), the emphatic pronoun niistóyi has the suffix yi, apparently because of the presence of the third person 'my son' as subject. In (x) kiistóyi is an "oblique" argument of the verb, linked by the prefix omoht 'source/means' (see section D.4 of chapter 16). The presence of the third person subject 'my friend' apparently requires the suffix yi on the pronoun. Similarly in (y), niistónnaani is linked by another variant (iiht) of the same prefix in a verb with a third person subject.

EXERCISES

1. **Given:**   **Translate:**
   a. niksíssta "my mother"   "our$_{21}$ mothers"
   b. otohpóósiimi "his cat"   "our$_{1p}$ cat"
   c. nohkátsi "my foot"   "his feet"
   d. katsiníwaawayi "your$_{2p}$ tongue"   "their tongues"
   e. kóta'sa "your$_{2s}$ mount"   "his$_{4s}$ mount"
   f. amo póósa "this cat"   "this cat's feet"

Possessives 77

2. The phrase <u>this</u> <u>cat's</u> <u>foot</u> is ambiguous in English, because <u>this</u> may modify either <u>cat</u> or <u>foot</u>; translate it into Blackfoot two ways, corresponding to the two meanings the English phrase can have. (See discussion in section F above.)

3. Given the following verb stems: <u>inihki</u> 'sing' (AI), <u>okska'si</u> 'run' (AI), and <u>ohkoono</u> 'find' (TA). Translate a.-c. into Blackfoot:

    a. Their mother is singing.

    b. Our$_{1p}$ mounts will run.

    c. The man's mother has found his dog.

CHAPTER FIFTEEN

Allomorphy

As alluded to in chapter 6, one of the few areas of irregularity in Blackfoot is the variation in shape of morphemes. By "irregularity" I mean variation other than that which is accounted for by regular phonological rules such as those presented in chapter 5.[92] Such irregular variation is referred to as "allomorphy", and the variant shapes of a single morpheme are called **allomorphs** of that morpheme. For Blackfoot, most of this variation is at the beginning of morphemes.

A. MORPHEME-INITIAL VARIATION

Initial variation can be grouped into several subtypes. Each of these is illustrated below.

∅ ~ I

A very large group of noun and verb roots which begin with a consonant when in word-initial position have an allomorph which begins with I if another morpheme is prefixed.[93] Here are some examples:[94]

---

[92]That is, **post-lexical** phonological rules. Much of the variation seen below would be accounted for in current theory by lexical phonological rules.

[93]The added vowel is sometimes referred to as "connective I".

[94]The situation has recently become even more complicated than the grouping presented here. E.g., for some speakers consulted on the Blood reserve, piitaa 'eagle' is Ipiitaa after omahk- 'big' but ohpiitaa after ksikk- 'white'.

Allomorphy

pookááwa	"child"	i'naks*i*pokaawa[95]	"infant"
náámayi	"bow"	sahks*i*náámayi	"short bow"
pi'kssííwa	"bird"	ómahks*i*pi'kssiiwa	"big bird/ turkey"
Píít!	"Enter!"	Áaks*i*piimma.	"She will enter."
Passkáát!	"Dance!"	Á*i*passkaayaawa.	"They are dancing."

Such morphemes are entered in the Dictionary under their consonant-initial allomorph if they are nouns, but under i otherwise.

Supplemental Material

A small subset of such roots lose a vowel after the first consonant, and that consonant assimilates to the following consonant to produce a long consonant:

ponokáwa	"elk"	siks*innoka*wa	"black elk"
kiipó	"ten"	kiip*íppo*	"one hundred"
kipitáaakiiwa	"old woman"	poks*íppitáaakii*wa	"little old woman"

See Thomson 1978 for discussion.

∅ ~ oh

Another large group of morphemes which begin with a consonant when in word-initial position have initial oh when a prefix is added. Here are a few examples:

kiááyowa	"bear"	siko*h*kiááyowa	"black bear"
póósa	"cat"	ómahko*h*poosa	"big cat"
kitsími	"doorway"	i'náko*h*kitsimi	"small doorway"
Po'kíoot!	"Follow!"	Áako*h*po'kioowa.	"She will follow."
Kókkit!	"Give it to me!"	Níto*h*kokkáyi.	"He gave it to me."
pokítapíwa	"small person"	iíko*h*pokitapiwa	"very small person"

These morphemes are also entered in the Dictionary under their consonant-initial allomorph if they are nouns, but with the oh present otherwise (though some prefixes are listed under their consonant-initial allomorph).

---

[95] See the discussion of Breaking in section A of chapter 6.

{m,n} ~ ∅

As stated in chapter 14, most morphemes which begin in a nasal (m or n) when in word-initial position lack this nasal when a prefix is added. Examples:

*n*atáyowa	"lynx"	ómahkatayowa	"mountain lion"
*m*á'sa	"Indian turnip"	ómahka'sa	"turnip"
*n*ínaawa	"man"	omahkínaawa	"old man"
*m*o'tsísi	"hand/arm"	ko'tsísi	"your hand/arm"
*N*inihkít!	"Sing!"	Áaksinihkiyaawa	"They will sing."

These morphemes are entered in the Dictionary with the initial nasal present unless they are verbs, in which case they are listed without the nasal.

Other fairly common alternations include the following:

i ~ o, a ~ o, and combinations of these with the nasal-loss alternation exibited above. Observe the following pairs:

*i*mitááwa	"dog"	sik*ó*mitaawa	"black dog"
*A*kstakít	"Count!"	Áak*o*kstakiwa	"She will count"
*ma*mííwa	"fish"	ksikk*o*mííwa	"white fish"
*ma*nistsíyi	"travois"	isttsik*ó*nistsiyi	"sled"
*a*kááni	"roping"	Nitáak*o*kaa	"I will rope"

Unless they are verb stems or roots, such morphemes are listed in the Dictionary in their word-initial form.[96]

B. VARIABLE-LENGTH VOWELS

The next alternation to be discussed in this chapter is not strictly limited to morpheme-initial position, but it is observed only in the first syllable of a morpheme. As first described by Taylor (1969), in addition to vowels which are always short and vowels which are always long, there are vowels which are either short or long depending upon their environment.

Here are examples with waanii ~ wanii "say":

---

[96]A very few stems have an apparent prefix w added before possessive prefixes (chapter 14) are added. *E.g.* compare nottoána 'my knife' to isttoána 'knife' and innísttoana 'long knife'. I take the form of 'knife' without a prefix to be IttoáN; see the rule s-Insertion in Appendix B.

Allomorphy 81

(a) áániiwa   "he said"
(b) áwaaniiwa   "he says"
(c) nitáánii ~ nitánii   "I said"
(d) nimáátaniihpa   "I didn't say"

Such vowels of variable length are always long if they are:

1. in the first syllable of a word, as in (a).[97]

2. preceded by a semivowel, in the same morpheme, that is not deleted by Semivowel Loss (see chapter 5), as in (b).[98]

3. preceded by the vowel i̱, as in (f) below. Length conditioned by the presence of the vowel i̱ is present even if the i̱ is deleted by i-Loss or i-Absorption.

If the only syllable preceding a variable length vowel is a person prefix (nit-, kit-, ot-), then the vowel may be either long or short, as in (c). In all other environments, variable length vowels are short, as in (d) and (e).

The direct theme suffix seen in chapter 10 is a variable length vowel; in (e) it is short, but in (f) it is long:

(e) nitsikákomimmawa   "I love her"
(f) nitá'kiaawa   "I hit him"

Variable length vowels will sometimes be listed as a̱:, o̱:, and i̱:.

C. MORPHEME-FINAL ALLOMORPHY

Irregular variation at the end of morphemes is far less common, but certain patterns can be identified.

Non-permanent consonants

The variation seen in chapter 2 at the end of nouns and abbreviated with symbols M̱, Ṉ, and S̱ is the most frequently encountered. A general statement about the realization of these abstract segments can be made:

---

[97] Occasionally such a vowel may be heard as short, but only if unaccented; e.g. aaníít ~ aníít 'say (something)!'

[98] It is a bit of a paradox that this allomorphy rule must make reference to the application of a phonological rule. This can be avoided only by writing the environment for Semivowel Loss into the rule for vowel length, as follows: "Such vowels are long if preceded by a semivowel which is itself not preceded by a consonant other than '."

M, N, and S are realized as m, n, and s, respectively, unless followed by a suffix which begins with a vowel, in which case they are realized as ∅ (*i.e.* null).

Here is an example of N before the glottal stop of the diminutive suffix:

aakííkoaN + 's + wa → aakííkoan'sa "poor little girl"

As was seen in chapter 2, and again in chapter 5, an initial semivowel of the following morpheme is dropped after the m, n, or s, as are all semivowels which would otherwise follow consonants.

Not only nouns exhibit such variation. There are a few intransitive verbs which exhibit an mm ~ ∅ alternation, and the forms with mm are precisely those with semivowel-initial suffixes. Here are some examples:

(g) áótsi**mm**a   "he swims"   *cf.* áótso'pa   "we$_{21}$ swim"
     á-otsiM:-wa   á-otsiM:-o'pa
     dur-swim-3s   dur-swim-21

(h) áaksipii**mm**ináyi   "she$_4$ will enter"   *cf.* kitáaksipii "you$_{2s}$ will enter"
     áak-IpiiM:-yini-áyi   kit-yáak-IpiiM:
     fut-enter-4s-PRO   2-fut-swim

This variation may be abbreviated by use of the symbol M:, as has been done in the morpheme-by-morpheme representation.

In the Dictionary, noun stems are listed with non-permanent consonants present, while verb stems are listed without the non-permanent mm.

Semivowel alternation

Another somewhat unusual morpheme-final variation is that seen in the following pairs of words:

(i) Kaayínnit!   "Hold it open!"
     Kaawáí'piksit!   "Open it!"

(j) iitsíyinamma   "it looks high quality"
     iikítsiwa'pssiwa[99]   "it is of good quality"

The alternation is between y and w; *i.e.* the morphemes involved (kaay ~ kaaw and itsiy ~ itsiw) end in a semivowel, but the quality of the semivowel

---

[99] The sequence Ciwa' will often sound like Co wa', as a result of the process called Coalescence 2 in a footnote in chapter 14.

is determined by the first vowel of the following morpheme:[100] if the following vowel is i or I, then the semivowel is y; otherwise, the semivowel is w.

In the Dictionary, such morphemes are listed as ending with a period (.).

Diphthongization

A number of stems ending in i, ii, or oo replace this i, ii, or oo with the diphthong ao before the 21 suffix o'p; observe the following:

(l) Itapáóo'pa. "We$_{21}$ went there." *cf.* Itapóówa. "He went there."
(m) Itáópaoo'pa. "We$_{21}$ stay there." *cf.* Itáópiiwa. "He stays there."
(n) Áakomáópaoo'pa. "We$_{21}$ will quiet down."
  cf. Áakomáópiiyaawa. "They will quiet down."
(o) Iipiksáó'pa. "We$_{21}$ hit (something)." *cf.* Iipiksíiwa. "He hit (s.t.)."

This diphthongization is not limited to the suffix -o'p of the independent paradigm. It also takes place with the 21 suffixes -o's and -o'k of the Conjunctive and Subjunctive paradigms; see chapter 19 and Appendix A regarding these paradigms.

---

[100] In current terminology, these morphemes end in a glide which is underspecified.

CHAPTER SIXTEEN

Complex Verb Stems, Part 1

One of the most salient features of Blackfoot is the complexity of its verb stems. Many morphemes, the closest equivalents of which are separate words in most other languages, are part of the verb in Blackfoot. These include negatives, quantifiers, intensifiers, all kinds of adverbials, and many, many others, including numerous morphemes which would be main or auxiliary verbs in other languages. In this chapter we will illustrate only a few of the morphemes which can make up complex stems. We will concentrate on morphemes (most of which are classed as "adjuncts" [*adt*] in the Dictionary) that do not determine the syntactic category of the stems of which they are a part; morphemes which do determine the syntactic category of the stems of which they are a part are discussed in chapters 17 and 18.

A. NEGATION

The negative prefix has five distinct forms; these occur in complementary distribution, as follows:[101]

máát- ~ Imá:t-

Used in verbs of independent clauses, if no prefix other than a person prefix precedes it in the verb:[102]

    Máátomáyo'kaawaiksaawa.   "They aren't asleep yet."
    máát-oma-yo'kaa-waiksaawa
    neg-yet-sleep-3p(nonaffirm)

---

[101] The symbol " ~ " is used to join variants of a single morpheme.

[102] Negated verbs of independent clauses generally occur with **non-affirmative** suffixes, discussed further in chapter 21. In the examples at hand, the non-affirmative affixes are -waiksaawa '3p' and -hpa '1s/2s'.

Nimáátáóoyihpa. "I'm not eating."
n-Imáát-á-ooyi-hpa
1-neg-dur-eat-nonaffirm

kátá'- ~ Ikátá'-

Used in verbs of the Unreal[103] paradigms (in contrary to fact clauses), if no prefix other than a person prefix precedes it in the verb:[104]

Kátá'yo'kaawahtopiyaawa, áaksstaayaawa mááhksoyssaawa.
kátá'-yo'kaa-wahtopi-yi-aawa yáak-sstaa-yi-aawa m-ááhk-Ioyi-hsi-aawa
neg-sleep-unreal-3p-PRO fut-want-3p-PRO 3-might-eat-conj-PRO[105]
"If they weren't asleep, they'd want to eat."

Nikátáí'naayihtopi, nitáakssakiaopii.
n-Ikátá'-inaa-yi-htopi nit-yáak-saki-a-opii
1-neg-chief-be-unreal 1-fut-still-dur-stay
"Were I not a chief, I'd still be home."

This last example requires presentation of an additional phonological rule. The negative prefix is listed as kátá'-, but the glottal stop of this prefix is positioned before the first consonant of the stem Inaayi 'be a chief'. This is a result of the following rule, which moves a morpheme-final glottal stop over a following vowel to the next consonant:

Glottal Metathesis

'+V → V' / _C

miin- ~ piin-

Used in imperative verb forms if not preceded by any other prefixes. (The variation between miin- and piin- is totally free.)

Miinasáí'nit./ Piinasáí'nit. "Don't cry!"
miin-wa:sai'ni-t
neg-cry-2s(imper)

---

[103]Called the "irrealis" in Uhlenbeck(1938). See chapter 19, section D.

[104]kátá'- is also used as an interrogative prefix in independent clauses, and as a negative prefix on nominalized verbs.

[105]New abbreviations in this section: 'conj' and 'subj' indicate affixes from the Conjunctive and Subjunctive paradigms, respectively (see chapter 19).

        Miinohkókkit. / Piinohkókkit.   "Don't give it to me!" .
        miin-ohkot-k-i-t
        neg-give(TA)-inv-1-2s(imper)

sta'-

Used only when preceded by the non-factive prefixes ááhk and á:k.[106]

    Kitsííksstato kááhksstai'pottaahsi.   "I want you to not fly."
    kit-iiksstat-o:k-ááhk-sta'-Ipottaa-hsi
    2-want(TA)-1:2 2-might-neg-fly-conj

    Kítssíímo,   kááksstai'sakssi.   "I forbid you to go out."
    kit-siim-o: k-áák-sta'-sa:ksi-hsi
    2-forbid(TA)-1:2 2-might-neg-exit-conj

say- ~ saw- ~ sa-

This variant of the verbal negator occurs elsewhere, *i.e.* in all environments other than those described above. It has the shape sa- if the following morpheme begins with a semivowel; it is say- if the following morpheme begins with i or I; elsewhere the prefix is saw-.

    Nitáakito'too sawomáóoyisaawa.[107]   "I'll arrive before they eat."
    nit-yáak-it-o'too saw-oma-ooyi-si-aawa
    1-fut-then-arrive neg-yet-eat-3(subj)-PRO

    Kítohkottssksiniihpa   áísawonawaissikópaoo'ssi.
    kit-ohkott-ssksini-hp-wa á-saw-onawa-ssikópao-o'ssi[108]
    2-able-know(TI)-theme-3s dur-neg-ever-rest-21(conj)
    "You should know we$_{21}$ never rest."

    Áakssayinakowa.   "It will be invisible."
    yáak-say-Inako-wa
    fut-neg-visible-3s

    Kítssksiniihpa nítssawáóoyssi.   "You know I'm not eating."
    kit-ssksini-hp-wa nit-saw-á-ooyi-hsi
    2-know(TI)-theme-3s 1-neg-dur-eat-conj

---

[106] sta'- is also used as an interrogative prefix, evidently as a non-initial variant of káta'- (see note above regarding káta'-): Áakstao'ohkaaniiwa? "Will she say (something)?"

[107] See section D.5 regarding prefix oma.

[108] See chapter 15, section C regarding 'diphthongization' of the stem ssikópii 'rest'.

Áakssawahkayiwaatsiksi.   "Will she not go home ?"
yáak-sa-wa:hkayi-waatsiksi
fut-neg-go^home-3s(nonaffirm)

Ikkámssawohkokkiiniki nitáakahkayi.
ikkám-saw-ohkot-kiiniki nit-yáak-wa:hkayi
if-neg-give(TA)-2:1(subj) 1-fut-go^home
"If you don't give it to me, I'll go home."

The last five examples point out the need for a phonological rule to account for the lengthening of morpheme-initial s when preceded by a morpheme which ends in a consonant other than glottal stop. We will call this **s-Connection a** because we will need a different rule (s-Connection b) for those cases in which the preceding morpheme ends in a vowel:[109]

s-Connection a

s → ss / C+_ , where C ≠ '

B. QUANTIFIERS

ohkan(a)- ~ kan(a)- 'all'[110]

Ómiksi pookáíksi áóhkanasai'niyaawa.   "Those kids are all cryers."
om-iksi pookáá-iksi á-ohkan-wa:sai'ni-yi-aawa
that-3p child-3p dur-all-cry-3p-PRO

Nitohkanáóhpommatoo'piaawa.   "I bought all of them."
nit-ohkana-ohpommatoo-'p-yi-aawa
1-all-buy(TI)-theme-ip-PRO

---

[109]This lengthening of s after consonants serves to distinguish t + s and k + s from the affricates ts and ks.

[110]It may be that we are dealing here with two closely related prefixes which differ in form only in that one ends in an a and the other does not. Compare this sentence to the following example:

Ómiksi pookáíksi áóhkanawaasai'niyaawa.   "Those kids all are capable of crying."
om-iksi pookáá-iksi á-ohkana-wa:sai'ni-yi-aawa
that-3p child-3p dur-all-cry-3p-PRO

And as Greg Thomson points out (personal communication), if ohkana ~ kana is a morpheme, it is discontinous in that other morphemes may intervene between the ohkan and the a; note the following example in which it- 'there' interrupts the past form of ohkana: iihkanítaipoyiyaawa "They all stood there."

Nitohkanáóhpommatoo'pinnaaniaawa. "We all bought them."/
nit-ohkana-ohpommatoo-'p-innaan-yi-aawa "We bought all of them."[111]
1-all-buy(TI)-theme-1p-ip-PRO

Iihkanáyo'kaayaawa. "They all slept."
iihkana-Io'kaa-yi-aawa
past:all-sleep-3p-PRO

The form kan(a)- is found primarily on nouns:

kanáítapiwa "all people"
kana-itapi-wa
all-person-3s

wayák- 'both/two'

Nitáyákohpommatoo'piaawa. "I bought both of them."
nit-wayák-ohpommatoo-'p-yi-aawa
1-both-buy(TI)-theme-ip-PRO

Nitáyákohpommatoo'pinnaaniaawa. "We both bought them."/
nit-wayák-ohpommatoo'p-innaan-yi-aawa "We bought both of them."[112]
1-both-buy(TI)-1p-ip-PRO

Áyákaisttsiistomiyaawa. "They are both sick."
wayák-a-isttsiistomi-yi-aawa
two-dur-sick(AI)-3p-PRO

C. VERBAL PREFIXES

These are prefixes the equivalents of which in most other languages would be verbs which take embedded clauses, as in the English translations below. Here are a few of the many such prefixes. (As stated in the introduction to this chapter, none of these determine the syntactic category of the stem of which they are a part.)

ohkott- 'able'

Kítohkottá'po'taki. "You were able to work."
kit-ohkott-a'po'taki
2-able-work

---

[111] Note that the 'all' may quantify either the plural subject or the plural object.

[112] Again, note that 'both' may quantify either the plural subject or the plural object.

Nimáátakohkottahkayihpa.   "I can't go home."
n-imáát-yak[113]-ohkott-wa:hkayi-hpa
1-neg-fut-able-go^home-nonaffirm

ssáak- 'try'

Aíssáaka'po'takiwa.   "He's trying to work."
á-ssáak-a'po'taki-wa
dur-try-work-3s

The preceding example illustrates what happens when a morpheme-initial s is preceded by a vowel. This is captured in the following rule:[114]

s-Connection b

$$\emptyset \to i / V(')+\_s, \quad \text{where } V \neq i$$

yaahs- 'like/enjoy/ be pleased by'

Nitáyaahsoyi.   "I like to eat."
nit-á-yaahs-Ioyi
1-dur-like-eat

Iksistt- 'finish'

Nikáíksisttsoyi.   "I've finished eating."
n-ikáá-Iksisst-Ioyi
1-perf-finish-eat

mato- ~ oto- 'go to do ...'

Iitóómiihkaawa.   "He went fishing."
iito-omii-hkaa-wa
past:go-fish-acquire-3s

Áakotaapinniiwa a'písiyi.   "He will go adjust the rope."
yáak-oto-apinn-ii-wa a'písi-yi
fut-go-adjust(TA)-dir-3s rope-4s

The preceding example indicates the need for yet another phonological rule.

---

[113]The future prefix, if that is what we have here, has a short vowel in this position.

[114]As shown in the rule, an intervening glottal stop does not block the insertion of i. See the second example under section D.2 of this chapter, in which s-Connection b feeds Glottal Metathesis.

Whenever a morpheme which ends in o is followed by a morpheme which begins with a, the o is replaced by a, as expressed in the following rule:[115]

o-Replacement

    o → a / _+a,   where +a is not a suffix

Note the condition stating that this rule does not apply if the a is part of a suffix, as in the following example:

Nítohpommoawa.   "I bought (something) for him."
nit-ohpomm-o-a:-wa
1-buy-ben(TA)-dir-3s

Here are two more examples of prefix mato- ~ oto-:

Áakotóooyo'pa.   "Let's go eat."
yáak-oto-ooyi-o'pa
fut-go-eat-21

Matóooyit.   "Go eat!"
mato-ooyi-t
go-eat-2s(imp)

Supplemental Material

The last two examples above illustrate a phonological rule which creates a falling pitch accent. Whenever a morpheme which ends in a vowel is followed by a morpheme which begins with a long vowel or diphthong (see chapter 1), a falling pitch is superimposed on the resultant vowel sequence. If the first vowel and the second vowel are identical, as in the preceding two examples, the pitch falls throughout the sequence. If the first and second vowel form a diphthong, accents are written over both the first vowel and the first vowel symbol of the long vowel:

Máátomáíiniitsiwaatsiksi.   "He hasn't drowned yet."
maat-oma-iiniitsi-waatsiksi
neg-yet-drown(AI)-3s:nonaffirm

Áípoináóokatakiwa.   "She's beading frantically."
á-Ipoina-ookataki-wa
dur-frantic-bead(AI)-3s

---

[115]For large groups of speakers, the o is deleted rather than replaced by a. For such speakers, "He will go adjust ..." would be Áakotapinniiwa ...

However, if the first vowel is i̱ and the second vowel is not i̱i̱, the falling pitch accent is assigned to the long vowel, whether or not the i̱ is subsequently lost:[116]

    aapániáakiiwa   "butterfly-woman"
    aapáni-aakii-wa
    butterfly-woman-3s

    paahtsáakiiwa   "mistaken-woman"
    paahtsi-aakii-wa
    mistake-woman-3s

The following examples demonstrate that this rule is not bled by o-Replacement:

    niipáaakiiwa   "upright woman"
    niipo-aakii-wa
    upright-woman-3s

    otahkáaokayiiwa   "robin"
    otahko-aokayii-wa
    orange-breat-3s

ohko- 'have for ...'

    Nítohkóooyi.   "I've got something to eat."
    nit-ohko-ooyi
    1-have^for-eat

    Nítohkaa'po'taki.   "I've got a job."
    nit-ohko-a'po'taki
    1-have^for-work

    Nikáóhkaayáámoyí'poyi   "I've got a joke (to tell)."
    n-ikáá-ohko-ayaamoyi'poyi
    1-perf-have^for-tell^joke(AI)

D. ADVERBIAL PREFIXES

1. Manner

Ikki̱na- 'gently/easy'

    Ikkináí'poyit!   "Speak slowly/clearly!"
    Ikkina-I'poyi-t
    gently-dur-speak-2s(imper)

---

[116]In addition to the expected loss of i̱ after s̱ (by i-Absorption) and after y̱ (by i-Loss), there is for many speakers loss of i̱ in these circumstances after ṉ. For example, piikáni + aakii 'Peigan woman' may be either piikániáakii or piikánáakii.

Nitsikkínaiksiinoka.   "She touched me gently."
nit-Ikkina-Iksiin-o:k-wa
1-gently-touch(TA)-inv-3s

iiyik- 'strong/hard'

Kitsííyika'po'taki.   "You worked hard."
kit-iiyik-a'po'taki
2-hard-work

Iiyíkssopowa.   "It's very windy."
iiyik-sopoo-wa
hard-wind-3s

póína- ~ Ipoina- 'nuisance/frenetic/erratic'

áípoináóoyiwa.   "He's eating frantically."
á-Ipoina-ooyi-wa
dur-frantic-eat-3s

Póínáóhkomatakiwa.   "He drives recklessly."
póína-ohkomataki-wa
reckless-drive-3s

Póínaa'pssiwa.   "He's a nuisance."
póína-a'pssi-wa
nuisance-be(AI)-3s

sok- 'well/good'

Kitsikáísoka'po'taki.   "You work very well."
kit-ik-á-sok-a'po'taki
2-very-dur-good-work

Máátáísokímohsiwaatsiksi.   "He's not feeling well."
máát-á-sok-imohsi-waatsiksi
neg-dur-good-feel-3s(nonaffirm)

Iíkssoka'pssiyaawa.   "They are good."
iik-sok-a'pssi-yi-aawa
very-good-be(AI)-3p-PRO

niit- ~ a:nist- 'manner'
>This prefix acts as a variable, with a range of values which includes the manner prefixes illustrated above. It is used in questions asking about manner (see chapter 21) and a type of nominalization (Conjunctive Nominals; see chapter 20). As will be seen in the following examples, this morpheme selects the short person prefixes.

>>niitáí'poyo'pi   "the way one speaks"
niit-á-I'poyi-o'p-yi
how-dur-speak-21:nom-in.s

>>kaanistáóoyihpi   "the way you eat"
k-aanist-á-ooyi-hp-yi
2-how-dur-eat-nom-in.s

>>niitáótso'pi   "how one swims / how we$_{21}$ swim"
niit-á-otsi-o'p-yi
how-dur-swim-21:nom-in.s

>>maanistáípasskaahpoaawaistsi   "the ways they dance"
m-aanist-á-Ipasskaa-hp-oaawa-istsi
3-how-dur-dance-nom-3p-ip

2. Degree

iik- 'very'

>Iiksíksistoyiwa.   "It's very hot."
iik-iksistoyi-wa
very-hot-in.s

sska'- 'extraordinarily'

>Isskáí'soka'piiwa.   "It's extraordinarily good."
isska'-sok-a'pii-wa
extra-good-be(II)-in.s

sstónnat- 'extremely' (literally "dangerously")

>Isstónnatsstoyiiwa.   "It's extremely cold."
isstónnat-sstoyii-wa
extreme-cold(II)-in.s

3. Rate

Ikkam- 'fast/quickly'

    Áíkkamokska'siwa.   "He runs fast."
    á-Ikkam-okska'si-wa
    dur-fast-run-3s

    Ikkamítsinikookit.   "Tell me about it quickly!"
    ikkam-itsiniko-o:kit
    quick-relate(TA)-2s:1s(imper)

iitsiksist- 'slow(ly)'

    Íítsiksistokska'siwa.   "He runs slowly."
    iitsiksist-okska'si-wa
    slow-run-3s

4. Linkers

These are prefixes which indicate the oblique grammatical relation of some nominal in the clause; they generally serve the same function as prepositions in English, except that because they are in the verb rather than adjacent to the related nominal, the hearer (or reader) must infer from context which nominal they link.[117]

omohp- ~ iihp- ~ ohp- 'associative'

The first variant of this prefix immediately follows person prefixes, the second variant occurs in word-initial position, and the latter elsewhere.[118]

    Napayíni nomohpiówatoo'pa ómihka í'ksisakoyihka.
    napayín-i n-omohp-Iowatoo-'p-wa om-yi-hka í'ksisako-yi-hka
    bread-nonpartic 1-assoc-eat(TI)-theme-3s that-in.s-invs meat-in.s-invs
    "I ate the meat **with** bread."

    Áakohpinnisiyaawa omi sináákia'tsisi.
    yáak-ohp-innisi-yi-aawa om-yi sináákia'tsiS-yi
    fut-assoc-fall-ip-PRO that-in.s book-in.s
    "They will fall **with** that book."

---

[117] Linkers are often called "relative roots" by Algonquianists.

[118] For some speakers the first variant has the form imohp-, and for still others it is o'ohp-. The same idiolectal variation is found in the first syllable of the next linker to be presented.

Complex Verb Stems, Part 1

omoht- ~ iiht- ~ oht- 'instrument(instr)/means/source/content/path'
The three variants of this prefix have a distribution parallel to the variants of the previous linker.

    Iihtáwayáakiaawa miistsíi.   "He was hit **with/by** a stick."
    iiht-wa:wayáaki-a:-wa miistsíS-i
    instr-hit(TA)-dir-3s stick-nonpartic

    Nitáakohtahkayi áípottaawa.   "I'll go home **by** plane."
    nit-yáak-oht-wa:hkayi áípottaa-wa
    1-fut-means-go^home plane-3s

    Nomohtó'too Lethbridge.   "I came **from** Lethbridge."
    n-omoht-o'too
    1-source-arrive

    Nómohtsitsinikooka kiistóyi.   "He told me (a story) **about** you."
    n-omoht-itsiniko-o:k-wa kiistóyi
    1-content-tell(TA)-inv-3s 2s(PRO)

    Iihtawááwahkaayaawa omíma niítahtaayi.
    iiht-a-wa:wakaa-yi-aawa om-yi-ma niítahtaa-yi
    along-dur-walk-3p-PRO that-in.s-stat river-in.s
    "They are walking **along** the river."

ohtahtsiwa- 'in place of/ in the stead of'

    Nohkówa otákkaayi iihtahtsówáóowatsiiwa[119] omi áaattsistaayi.
    n-ohkó-wa w-itákkaa-yi iihtahtsiwa-oowat-yii-wa om-yi áaattsistaa-yi
    1-son-3s 3-partner-4s past:in^place^of-eat(TA)-dir-3s that-4s rabbit-4s
    "My son **in place of** his partner ate the rabbit."

The remainder of the linkers to be listed, in addition to their linking function, add directional or spatial information. The first two occur in verbs which describe motion, or at least imply change of location, and indicate the direction of that motion or movement. The other may occur in just about any verb.

itap- 'toward'

    Nitáakitapoo kookóówayi.   "I'll go to your place."
    nit-yáak-itap-oo k-ookóówa-yi
    1-fut-toward-go 2-home-in.s

---

[119]Coalescence 2 accounts for the o̲ in the third syllable of this verb. See the third footnote of chapter 14.

While no overt nominal is linked by the following directional prefix, it is grouped here because it can be viewed as linking location of the speaker:

poohsap- ~ Ipoohsap- 'toward location of the speaker'

    Póóhsapoot!   "Come here!"
    póóhsap-oo-t
    toward^spkr-go-2s(imper)

    Áaksipoohsapokska'siwa.   "He'll run toward me."
    yáak-Ipoohsap-okska'si-wa
    fut-toward^spkr-run-3s

it- ~ ist-[120] 'there'

    Itáóoyiwa nookóówayi.   "He eats at my place."
    it-yá-ooyi-wa n-ookóówa-yi
      there-dur-eat(AI)-3s 1-home-in.s

    Anni istópiit!   "Sit there!"
    ann-yi ist-opii-t
    that-in.s there-sit-2s(imper)

5. Aspect

There are additional prefixes which fit under the label 'aspect', as that term is defined in chapter 6. Here are a few:

saaki- ~ saki-[121] 'still'

    Saakiáítapiwa.   "She's still living."
    saaki-á-itapi-wa
    still-dur-live-3s

    Nimáátssakiáíssksiniihpa.   "I don't remember."
    n-imáát-saki-á-ssksini-hp-wa
    1-neg-still-dur-know(TI)-theme-in.s

---

[120]The second variant apparently is used only in imperatives.

[121]See section B of chapter 15 regarding this variation in vowel length.

omá- ~ iimá- 'yet'

    Kikátao'máóoyihpa?[122]   "Did you eat yet?"
    k-Ikáta'-omá-ooyi-hpa
    2-interrog-yet-eat-nonaffirm

    Iimáítsskaayaawa.   "They're fighting yet."
    iimá-itsskaa-yi-aawa
    yet-fight-3p-PRO

á'- 'inchoative' ('has just come about')[123]

    Nitáó'mai'taki.   "*Now* I'm convinced."
    nit-á'-omai'taki
    1-inchoat-believe   (*cf.* Nitáómai'taki. "I believe.")

    Áí'too'toowa   nááto'kaayi.   "It's two o'clock."
    a'-it-o'too-wa   naato'kaayi
    inchoat-there-arrive-in.s two

6. Non-linking Locationals

The following locational prefixes might, in view of their meaning, appear to be linkers, but notice that if a nominal is linked in these examples, there is an additional linker it- ~ ist- 'there' in the verb.

ípsst- 'inside'

    Itsípsstsoyo'pa omí ksikkokóówayi.   "We ate inside the tent."
    it-ipsst-Ioyi-o'pa om-yi ksikkokóówa-yi
    there-inside-eat(AI)-21 that-in.s tent-in.s

---

[122] Many speakers regularly reduce the sequence kikáta'- to kíta'-, so this will commonly be heard as kítao'máóoyihpa.

[123] Greg Thomson (personal communication) finds that one discourse function of this prefix is to indicate that the event expected at that point in the discourse did indeed occur.

ohkit- 'upon'

    Istohkítsstoota   omi akssíni.   "Put it on the bed!"
    ist-ohkit-ihtoo-t om-yi akihsíN-yi
    there-upon-put(TI)-2s(imper) that-in.s bed-in.s

    Matsíwohkitopiiwa.[124]   "He is a rider of a fine horse."
    matsíw-ohkit-opii-wa
    fine-upon-sit-3s

miistap- ~ yIIstap- 'away'

    Iyíístapokska'siwa.   "He ran away."
    i-yíístap-okska'si-wa
    past-away-run-3s

    Áaksiistapsskoyiiwáyi.   "She will chase him away."
    yáak-yIIstap-ssko-yii-wa-áyi
    fut-away-chase(TA)-dir-3s-PRO

The next example might also seem to involve linking of a nominal, but the nominal <u>annoma</u> 'here' is the object of a transitive verb:

    Míístapáaatoot annóma!   "Go away from here!"
    míístap-áaatoo-t annoma
    away-go(TI)-2s(imper) here

---

[124]Pronounced [matsówohkitopiiw]; see Coalescence 2 in note of section C of chapter 14. <u>ohkit+opii</u> is an idiom for 'ride (a horse)'

CHAPTER SEVENTEEN

Complex Verb Stems, Part 2: Finals

As alluded to in chapter 16, there are morphemes in complex stems which determine the syntactic category of the stem of which they are a part. We will designate as the **Head** of a stem that portion which determines the syntactic category of the entire stem. Because these are generally referred to as **finals** in Algonquian studies,[125] they will be referred to by that term here. The relevant syntactic categories determined by verb finals are primarily the four stem types discussed in chapter 7, *i.e.* transitive animate (TA), transitive inanimate (TI), animate intransitive (AI), and inanimate intransitive (II).

It will be useful to distinguish **simplex verb stems**, which consist of root plus final, and **complex verb stems**, which are made up of a stem (which itself may be complex) plus any or all of the following: preverbal elements such as those discussed in chapter 16, medials (follow a root and usually refer to body parts), and finals. In each complex stem, the rightmost final is the Head.

There are two broad classes of verb finals: "abstract" finals, which only minimally affect the meaning of the stem to which they are added, and "concrete" finals, which contribute significantly to the meaning of the stem. The remainder of this chapter will deal sketchily with the former type. Such finals, unlike concrete finals, are not "productive"; *i.e.*, they cannot be used freely to make up new stems. This means that which finals go with which roots is not predictable, and so the stems which have these finals must be learned as a whole.

Consider the verb stems of the following three sentences:

(a) Nitá-ooy-*i* (paatáki). "I'm eating (potatoes)."
(b) Nitá-oow-*atoo*'pi amostsi paatákistsi. "I'm eating these potatoes."
(c) Nitá-oow-*at*aawa amo pi'kssíiwa. "I'm eating this chicken."

---

[125]See Bloomfield 1946, p. 104.

The portion (here preceded and followed by hyphens for ease of exposition) common to all of these stems is a verb **root**.[126] Only a few verb roots can alone serve as a verb stem;[127] most, like that above, must occur with a final. The stems in (a)-(c) differ from each other in that they end in different finals (highlighted).[128] And as was stated above, the final determines the syntactic category of the stem. So the final in (a) determines that the verb stem is AI; consequently that stem occurs in an intransitive clause, *i.e* one with no object unless that object is non-particular (recall from section C of chapter 7 that objects which are non-particular in reference do not count as objects for purposes of verb transitivity in Blackfoot). Likewise, the the finals in (b) and (c) determine that the stems of these two examples are TA and TI, respectively, and occur in transitive clauses.

There are many roots which, like the one in (a)-(c), can occur with different finals. Here is another set of three sentences with verbs that share a common root, but this particular root selects different finals to form AI, TA, and TI stems:

(d) Kitá-omai't-*aki*hpoaawa.   "You$_{2p}$ believe."
(e) Kitá-omai't-*oo*'poaawa.   "You$_{2p}$ believe it."
(f) Kitá-omai't-*o*aawaayi kóko'soaawaiksi.   "You$_{2p}$ believe your kids."

The six finals seen in (a) - (c) above are all very common, and there are many other verb finals which are found in numerous stems.

Stems do not always occur in triples, like the preceding two sets. Many roots occur with only one or two different finals.

Here are some verb stem sets exhibiting some of the many common finals (finals are in bold print). The first three sets, like those above, are made up of AI, TI, and TA stems:

(g) Anna pookááwa áók*staki*wa.   "The child is counting/reading."

(h) Anna pookááwa áók*stoo*ma omistsi paatákistsi.
    "The child is counting those potatoes."

(i) Anna pookááwa áóks*i*yiiwa omiksi pi'kssííksi.
    "The child is counting those birds."

---

[126] The root in these cases exhibits semivowel alternation (see chapter 15); *i.e.*,it is <u>ooy</u> ~ <u>oow</u>.

[127] Even for these, it is useful to say that they have "zero" (null) finals.

[128] As can be seen by comparing even the few sets of finals in this chapter, the finals themselves can be further analyzed.

Complex Verb Stems, Part 2

(j) Nitán*ii*. "I said (something)."
(k) Nitán*istoo*'pa. "I said it."
(l) Nitán*ista*awa. "I told him."

(m) Kitáísína*aki* "You are drawing."
(n) Kitáísína*ii*'pa "You are drawing it."
(o) Kitáísínaoka[129] "He is taking your picture."

The next sets are AI/II pairs:

(p) Soká'ps*si*wa "She is good."
(q) Soká'p*ii*wa "It is good."

(r) Náa*i*yaawa "They (anim) are six.
 (*i.e.* there are six of them)."
(s) Náa*o*yaawa "They (inan) are six."

(t) Itsim*ímm*a[130] "He stinks."
(u) Itsímówa "It stinks."

The next two sets involve what are known as **instrumental finals**, because they indicate the instrument (usually a body part) involved. In (v) - (x), the instrument is the mouth.

(v) Nítssiksi*p*awa "I bit him." (TA)
(w) Nítssiks*stsii*hpa "I bit it." (TI)
(x) Nitssíks*staki*[131] "I bit (something)." (AI)

(y) Kitsíípoks*sko*awa "You smashed him with your foot." (TA)
(z) Kitsíípoks*ski*hpiaawa "You smashed them with your foot." (TI)

---

[129]This stem has a zero final.

[130]The mm is from M:; see section C of chapter 15.

[131]Note that the AI final a:ki is added to the TI final less the portion ii which is common to most TI stems).

CHAPTER EIGHTEEN

Some Concrete Finals

This chapter describes the formation of complex stems in which the Head is a derivational suffix; *i.e.* a suffix which changes the syntactic category of the stem to which it is added. As with the finals discussed in the previous chapter, the relevant syntactic categories are TA, TI, AI and II, but also make reference to the potential for occurrence with unlinked nominals (see section D.4 of chapter 16 regarding linkers).

Underlying versus surface grammatical relations

For purposes of this discussion, the underlying subject or object of a derived stem is the nominal which would have been subject or object of that stem were the derivational suffix not present. The surface subject or object of a stem is that for which that stem (whether basic or derived) is subcategorized (see section B of chapter 7).

A. CAUSATIVE VERB STEMS

There are two suffixes, <u>áttsi</u> and <u>pi</u>~<u>ipi</u>, which derive causative verb stems from other verb stems.[132] These suffixes are added to intransitive stems, never to transitive stems. The derived causative stem is transitive (unless the subject of the underlying non-causative verb is non-particular or unspecified - see below). Causative stems are used in clauses in which the causer is subject and the causee, which in all cases is understood as the subject of the underlying

---

[132]There is another suffix which, in all the examples available to me, is added to meteorological verbs to form AI verbs:

(i) Isopó***msst***aawa "He made the wind blow."
(ii) Nitáakssota***msstaa*** "I'll make it rain."

non-causative clause, is the primary object. For example, in (a) first person singular is the causer, and hence subject, and 'my daughter' is the causee, and hence primary object.

   (a) Nítsspiyáttsaawa nitána.   "I made my daughter dance."
       nit-ihpiyi-áttsi-a:-wa n-itán-wa
       1-dance(AI)-cause-dir-3s my-da-3s

Here are more examples of the two causative suffixes:

   (b) Kitsó'kááttsaayaawa.   "You put them to sleep."
       kit-Io'kaa-áttsi-a:-yi-aawa
       2-sleep(AI)-cause-dir-3p-PRO

   (c) Nitáókska'síípiooka.   "He makes me run."
       nit-á-okska'si-ipi-o:k-wa
       1-dur-run(AI)-cause-inv-3s

   (d) Kítso'káápiaayaawa.   "You put them to sleep."
       kit-Io'kaa-pi-a:-yi-aawa
       2-sleep(AI)-cause-dir-3p-PRO

The limitation that these two causative suffixes are added to **intransitive** stems is a morphological property of the causative suffixes themselves, not a consequence of their meaning. So they may be used whether or not the underlying non-causative clause has an object. However, if there is an underlying object, it will be a surface secondary object:

   (e) Nítohpommááttsaawa nohkówa omiksi ápotsskinaiksi.
       nit-ohpommaa-áttsi-a:-wa n-ohkó-wa om-iksi ápotskina-iksi
       1-buy(AI)-cause-dir-3s my-son-3s that-3/4p cow-3/4p
       "I made my son buy those cows."

Notice that the verb agrees with 'son$_{3s}$' as primary object, not with the underlying object, 'those cows$_{4p}$', which is the surface secondary object.

Supplemental Material

If the underlying subject of the stem is non-particular or unspecified, in which case it cannot be a surface primary object (see section C of chapter 7), the causative verb stem must be made intransitive by addition of the final a:ki,[133] which forms AI verbs:

---

[133] Also seen in (d), (g), (m), and (x) of chapter 17.

(f) Nítohpommááttsaaki (aakííkoai) napayíni.   "I caused (girl) buying of bread."
    nit-ohpommaa-áttsi-a:ki (aakííkoaN-i) napayín-i
    1-buy(AI)-cause-fin(AI) (girl-nonpartic) bread-nonpartic

We stated above that the causative finals are always added to intransitive stems. While this is true, the stem to which they are added is not always the usual intransitive stem. For example, the regular AI stem for 'beckon, make signs' is a'psstaki; yet the stem to which the causative suffixes are added is a'psstoyi, as seen in (g) and (h):

(g) A'psstoyáttsiyiiwáyi.   "He made him talk sign language."
    a'psstoyi-áttsi-yii-wa-áyi
    make^signs-cause-3:4-3s-PRO

(h) A'psstoyíípiyiiwáyi.   "He made him talk sign language."
    a'psstoyi-ipi-yii-wa-áyi
    make^signs-cause-3:4-3s-PRO

B. BENEFACTIVE VERB STEMS

Transitive stems which have a benefactee as primary object are derived from other stems by addition of one of two suffixes: -o and -mo ~ omo. Though the facts are complicated (see Taylor 1969, section 670 and 694), the following rough summary of their distribution may be of value.

The first of the two benefactive suffixes (-o) seems to be added to verb roots; compare the following non-benefactive and benefactive sentence pairs:

(j) 1. Iihpómmaawa ónnikii.   "He bought milk."
       iihpomm-aa-wa ónnikiS-i
       buy-AI-3s milk-nonpartic

    2. Iihpómmoyiiwáyi ónnikii.   "He bought milk for her."
       iihpomm-o-yii-wa-ayi ónnikiS-i
       buy-ben(TA)-dir-3s-PRO milk-nonpartic

(k) 1. Nítsskiitatoo'piaawa.   "I baked them."
       nit-ihkiit-watoo-'p-yi-aawa
       1-bake-TI-theme-ip-PRO

    2. Nítsskiitoawaistsi nitána.   "I baked them for my daughter."
       nit-ihkiit-o-a:-wa-aistsi n-itán-wa
       1-bake-ben(TA)-dir-3s-PRO 1-daughter-3s

For all benefactives, an underlying object (if any) will be the surface secondary object. So the pronoun for the baked items, which is the primary object in 1. of (k), is the secondary object in 2.

The suffix -mo ~ omo is usually added to transitive stems (mo after vowels, omo after consonants); in particular, it is added to what generally appear to be TA stems, as illustrated in the following examples of TA and benefactive pairs:

(l) 1. Kóta'siksi nitsííyissksipistayaawa.   "I tied up your horses."
k-ota's-iksi nit-ii-yIssksipist-a:-yi-aawa
2-mount-3p 1-past-tie^up(TA)-dir-3p-PRO

2. Nitsííyissksipistomoawa nitákkaawa óta'siksi.
nit-ii-yIssksipist-omo-a:-wa n-itákkaa-wa w-óta's-iksi
1-past-tie-ben(TA)-dir-3s 1-partner-3s 3-mount-4p
"I tied his horses up for my partner."

Observe that in 1. of (l) the being which is tied up is the primary object, while in 2. it is the secondary object.

(m) 1. Anna ponokáwa kitáaksinnootatawaatsiksi?
ann-wa ponoká-wa kit-yáak-Innootat-a:-waatsiksi
that-3s elk-3s 2-fut-butcher(TA)-dir-3s(nonaffirm)
"Will you butcher that elk?"

2. Kitáaksinnootatomookihpaatsiksi?   "Will you butcher him for me?"
kit-yáak-Innootat-omo-o:k-i-hp-waatsiksi
2-fut-butcher-ben(TA)-inv-2:1-nonaffirm-PRO

Supplemental Material

There are many cases where the suffix -mo~omo is added to other than the TA stem. *E.g.*, in the following example, it is added to the AI stem, less what looks like the AI final aa; but we cannot say -omo is added to a root in this case, for the corresponding TA stem (sstaahka), which presumably is based on the same root, lacks the ht portion:

(n) 1. Aísstaahkahtaawa   "She is nursing."
á-sstaahkahtaa-wa
suckle(AI)-3s

2. Nitsstááhkahtomoka nítsssitsimaani.   "She nursed my baby for me."
nit-sstaahkaht-omo-o:k-wa nit-ssitsimaan-yi
1-suckle-ben(TA)-inv-3s 1-baby-4s

And it is not clear what stem the benefactive suffix is attached to in 3. of (o); compare the stems of 1. and 2.:

(o) 1. Nitáaksipíiksaawa.   "I will chop it (animate gender)."
nit-yáak-IpíikI-a:-wa
1-fut-chop(TA)-dir-3s

2. Nitáaksipíiksii'pa.   "I will chop it (inanimate gender)."
nit-yáak-IpíikII-'p-wa
1-fut-chop(TI)-theme-3s

3. Kitáaksipíiksóomoo.   "I will chop (wood) for you."

C. ACCOMPANIMENT VERB STEMS

Another final which, like the causative finals of section A, is always added to an intransitive verb stem, is the accompaniment suffix -:m. (The colon here represents the fact that this suffix causes lengthening of a preceding short vowel.) Unique to this final,[134] however, is that it requires preverbal element ohpok- on the same verb. The resulting stem is transitive animate, and both its subject and primary object are understood as logical subjects of the underlying verb. For example, to animate intransitive stem a'po'taki 'work' there corresponds TA stem ohpoka'po'takiim 'work with'. So in the following example, both the surface subject nitána and the surface primary object nohkóyi are understood as participating in some work, but the sentence additionally includes the information that nitána has initiated the accompaniment of nohkóyi in the work.[135]

(p) Nitána iihpoká'po'takiimiiwa nohkóyi.
n+itán+wa iihpok+a'po'taki+:m+yii-wa n-ohko-yi
1-daughter-3s past:accomp-work(AI)-TA-3:4-3s 1-son-4s
"My daughter worked with my son."

Here are more examples of this construction:

(q) Nítohpokohto'toomaw amá nitohkíímaana Omahkoyisi.
nit-ohpok-oht-o'too-:m'a:'wa am-wa nit-ohkiimaan-wa omahk-oyiS-yi
1-accomp-source-arrive-TA'dir'3s this-3s 1-wife-3s big-lodge-in.s
"I arrived from Edmonton with my wife."

---

[134]Here I am assuming that the suffix -:m seen here should not be identified with the TA final -m seen in stems such as i'tsskaam 'fight'(TA); cf. i'tsskaa 'fight'(AI).

[135]Actually, the situation is not this clear. The motivation for choosing which member of the set understood as underlying subject to make the surface subject is as subtle as the choice made by English speakers utilizing the English equivalents of such Blackfoot sentences.

(r) Nítohpokihpiyiimoka oma aakííkoana.
   nit-ohpok-ihpiyi-:m-o:k-wa om-wa aakiikoaN-wa
   1-accomp-dance-TA-inv-3s that-3s-girl-3s
   "That girl danced with me."

An underlying object of the verb will be a surface secondary object, as illustrated in (s), where <u>omi áaattsistaayi</u> is the secondary object:

(s) Anna nohkówa, nítohpoksoyiimaawa omi áaattsistaayi.
   ann-wa n-ohko-wa nit-ohpok-Ioyi-:m-a:-wa om-yi áaattsistaa-yi
   that-3s 1-son-3s 1-accomp-eat-TA-dir-3s that-4s rabbit-4s
   "I ate that rabbit with my son."

D. REFLEXIVE VERB STEMS

Addition of final -<u>o:hsi</u> to TA stems produces AI stems which describe actions in which the subject of the resultant AI verb is understood as both underlying subject and underlying object. (See section B of chapter 15 regarding variable length vowels such as <u>o:</u>.) For example, the subject of (t) is understood as both the one who did the shooting and the one who was shot:

(t) Isskonákatohsiwa.   "He shot himself."
   i-sskonákat-o:hsi-wa
   past-shoot(TA)-refl(AI)-3s

Here are more examples:

(u) Nitáínoohsspinnaan.   "We$_{1p}$ see ourselves."
   nit-á-Ino-o:hsi-hpinnaan
   1-dur-see(TA)-refl(AI)-1p

(v) Oma imitááwa siiksípohsiwa.   "That dog bit himself."
   om-wa imitáá-wa siiksip-o:hsi-wa
   that-3s-dog-3s past:bite(TA)-refl(AI)-3s

(w) Sstsipísoohsit!   "Punish (whip) yourself!"
   sstsipísi-o:hsi-t
   whip(TA)-refl(AI)-2s(imper)

E. RECIPROCAL VERB STEMS

Addition of the final -<u>o:tsiiyi</u> ~ -<u>tsiiyi</u> to TA stems forms AI stems which describe reciprocal action between members of a set as subject. (The variant without initial <u>o:</u> occurs after stems ending in <u>t</u>.) So, for example, each of the horses mentioned in (x) is understood to both bite and be bitten by at least one of the other horses.

(x) Omiksi ponokáómitaiksi áísiksipotsiiyiyaawa.
   om-iksi ponokáómitaa-iksi á-siksip-o:tsiiyi-yi-aawa
   that-3p horse-3p dur-bite(TA)-recipr(AI)-3p-PRO
   "Those horses are biting each other."

(y) Anniksi kitómitaamiksi áíssáaksi'nittsiiyiyaawa.
   ann-iksi kit-omitaam-iksi á-ssáak-I'nit-tsiiyi-yi-aawa
   those-3p 2-dog-3p dur-try-kill(TA)-recipr(AI)-3p-PRO
   "Your dogs are trying to kill each other."

There is also a TA reciprocal final -o:tsiim ~ -tsiim, used apparently when the speaker wishes to ascribe responsibility for initiating the reciprocal action to one party, which is then the subject of the TA verb:

(z) Otáwáa'psskattsiimoka nohkówa ómi nínaayi.
   ot-á-wáa'psskat-tsiim-ok-wa n-ohkó-wa nínaa-yi
   3-dur-bet(TA)-recipr(TA)-inv-3s 1-son-3s man-4s
   "That man is betting my son."

F. DENOMINAL VERBS

There are finals which form verbs when added to noun stems. Four are presented here.

-wa'si 'become, turn into'

    Aakííkoana'siwa. "She turned into a girl."
    aakiikoaN-wa'si-wa
    girl-become-3s

    nítohkiááyowa'si "I became enraged
    nit-ohkiááyo-wa'si (lit: I became a bear)"
    1-bear-become

-hkaa ~ -Ihkaa 'acquire'

    Iimííhkaayaawa. "They fished
    iimii-hkaa-yi-aawa (lit: acquired fish)."
    past:fish-acqu(AI)-3p-PRO

    Nitsináánsskaa. "I got something."
    nit-inaan-Ihkaa
    1-possession-acqu(AI)

    Nitsíítsikiihkaa. "I got shoes"
    nit+iitsitsikiN+Ihkaa
    1-past:shoe-acqu(AI)

Some Concrete Finals

-hko ~ -Ihko 'provide for'
    This is the transitive animate counterpart to the preceding final.

    Nitsináánsskoayaawa.   "I got something for them."
    nit-inaan-Ihko-a:-yi-aawa
    1-possession-provide(TA)-dir-3p-PRO

-yi ~ -∅ 'be'
    As stated in section D of chapter 4, the null allomorph of this suffix is used only with a third person subject in an independent clause.

    Kitaínayihpoááwa?   "Are you chiefs?"
    kit-á-Ina[136]-yi-hpoaawa
    2-dur-chief-be-2p(nonaffirm)

    Nínaawa.   "He is a man/chief."
    nínaa-∅-aawa
    man/chief-be-3s

    Ikkamínayisi, nomohtsííksipisatsi'taki.
    ikkam-Ina-yi-si n-omoht-iik-Ipisatsi'taki
    if-chief-be-3(subj) 1-means-very-amazed
    "If he's a chief, I'm amazed."

---

[136]The stems for 'chief' and 'man' both have allomorphs which end in a short vowel when followed by a non-null derivational suffix.

CHAPTER NINETEEN

Other Verb Paradigms

The verb paradigms which have been presented thus far are used only in **independent** (main) clauses. This chapter describes verb forms used in subordinate clauses (sections A and B) and in commands (section C).

There are two sets of verb paradigms used in subordinate clauses, the **Conjunctive**[137] and the **Subjunctive**. As will be illustrated below, which of these two sets of paradigms is used in a dependent clause is determined by the content of that clause, the Subjunctive appearing in what can be characterized as clauses which are "presumptive" or "conditional" in meaning.

The Conjunctive paradigm set is the simpler to describe in that it is closely related to the set of verb paradigms in independent clauses, which have been presented in earlier chapters. Roughly, the Conjunctive paradigms differ from the corresponding Independent paradigms by the presence of an hs and a suffix yi. The hs immediately follows the verb stem in AI and II stems; in TA and TI verbs it follows the theme suffix. The suffix yi is last in the verb, preceded by any agreement suffixes. Another significant difference is that third person is marked by a prefix ot ~ w.

The Subjunctive paradigms show more extensive differences from the Independent paradigms, including the lack of person prefixes. Both the Conjunctive and the Subjunctive paradigm sets lack distinctive suffixes for minor third person.

Each paradigm from each set is exemplified in the next two sections of this chapter. The complete paradigms are presented in Appendix A.

---

[137]Called the **Conjunct** in earlier works such as Frantz 1971.

A. THE CONJUNCTIVE PARADIGMS

Clauses which call for verb forms from this set are the following:[138]

1. Temporal clauses of past occurrence; note that the verb contains prefix á', glossed 'inchoat(ive)':

   (a) Áyo'kaawa nitáí'to'toohsi.
   á-Io'kaa-wa nit-á'-it-o'too-hs-yi
   dur-sleep(AI)-3s 1-inchoat-there-arrive(AI)-conj-conj
   "He was asleep when I got there."

   (b) Nitáísskskammawa kitá'waawayákiyssi.
   nit-á-sskskamm-a:-wa kit-á'-wa:wayaki-yi-hs-yi
   1-dur-watch(TA)-dir-3s 2-inchoat-hit(TA)-inv-conj-conj
   "I was watching over her when she hit you."

2. Purpose clauses; the Conjunctive verb includes prefix ááhk 'non-factive',[139] and the verb of the independent clause in such cases usually includes the 'means/source' oblique linker iiht- ~ oht- ~ -omoht [see chapter 16]:

   (c) Nomohtó'too kááhksspommookssoaayi.
   n-omoht-o'too k-ááhk-sspommo-o:k-i-hs-oaa-yi
   1-source-arrive(AI) 2-might-help(TA)-inv-1-conj-2p-conj
   "I came for you$_{2p}$ to help me."

   (d) Kitáakohtsstsisóóhpa kááhkitáóhpommaahsi?
   kit-yáak-oht-ihtsisoo-hpa k-ááhk-it-á-ohpommaa-hs-yi
   2-fut-source-go^town-nonaff 2-might-there-dur-buy-conj-conj
   "Are you going to town to shop?"

3. Embedded clauses:

   a. As subject:

   (e) Íikssoka'piiwa otáísootaahsi. "It's good that it is raining."
   iik-soka'pii-wa ot-á-sootaa-hs-yi
   very-good(AI)-in.s 3-dur-rain(II)-conj-conj

---

[138]'conj' abbreviates 'Conjunctive'.

[139]The prefix ááhk 'non-factive' appears here with the short allomorphs of the person agreement prefixes (see chapter 6, section D.). For many speakers on the Blood Reserve this morpheme selects the long allomorphs.

b. As primary object:

(f) Nítssksinii'pa kitsówatoohsoaayi. "I know you ate it."
nit-ssksini-'p-wa kit-Iowatoo-hs-oaa-yi
1-know(TI)-theme-in.s 2-eat(TI)-conj-2p-conj

c. As secondary object:

(g) Nitánikkoowa kitsikákomimmahsi nitána.
nit-wa:nIt-k-oowa kit-ik-akomimm-a:-hs-yi n-itán-wa
1-tell(TA)-inv-unspec 2-very-love(TA)-dir-conj-conj 1-da.-3s
"I was told that you love my daughter."

(h) Iimáí'takiyaawa kitá'pistotsi'si ámoyi.
iimai'taki-yi-aawa kit-á'pistotsi-'s-yi amo-yi
pst:believe(AI)-3p-PRO 2-make(TI)-conj-conj this-in.s[140]
"They believed that you made this."

d. As complement of 'want'; observe that <u>ááhk</u> is used here as well:[141]

(i) Nitsíksstaa nááhksoyssi. "I want to eat."
nit-ik-sstaa n-ááhk-Ioyi-hs-yi
1-very-want(AI) 1-might-eat(AI)-conj-conj

e. As linked oblique, especially as non-suppositional cause of a main clause consequent; observe that in (j) and (k) the consequent contains the 'source' oblique linker:

(j) Nitsíkohtaahsí'taki kikáó'toohsi.
nit-ik-oht-yaahs-i'taki k-ikáá-o'too-hs-yi
1-very-source-good-feel(AI) 2-perf-arrive(AI)-conj-conj
"I'm glad that you have arrived."

(k) Iihtokí'takiyaawa nikáóowatoohsinnaani
iiht-ok-i'taki-yi-aawa n-ikáá-oowatoo-hs-innaan-yi
source-bad-feel-3p-PRO 1-perf-eat(TI)-conj-1p-conj

otsskíítaanoaawaistsska.
ot-ihkiitaa-n-oaawa-istsi-hka
3-bake(AI)-nom-3p-ip-invs

"They are angry because we have eaten their pastries."

---

[140] A colon is used in glosses when more than one category is represented in a single morpheme.

[141] More examples may be found in section C of chapter 22.

B. THE SUBJUNCTIVE PARADIGMS

Clauses which call for verb forms from this set are the following:[142]

1. Suppositional antecedent (an "if" clause) for a consequent expressed as the main clause; the Subjunctive verb in such clauses will usually have prefix ikkam 'if':

(l) Ikkamáyo'kainoainiki, nitáakahkayi.
   ikkam-á-yo'kaa-inoainiki nit-yáak-wa:hkayi
   if-dur-sleep(AI)-2p(subj) 1-fut-go^home
"If you$_{2p}$ are sleeping, I'll go home."

(m) Ikkamínimmiinnaaniki, nitáaksowatoo'pinnaana.
   ikkam-Ini-mmiinnaaniki nit-yáak-Iowatoo-'p-innaan-wa
   if-see(TI)-1p(subj)   1-fut-eat(TI)-theme-1p-in.s
"If we see it, we'll eat it."

(n) Ikkámssawohkókkiiniki, annáhka nínnahka áaksskoʼtsimáyi.
   ikkam-saw-ohkot-kiiniki ann-wa-hka n-inn-wa-hka yáak-ssk-o'tsi-m-wa-áyi
   if-neg-give(TA)-2s:1p(subj) this-3s-invs 1-fa-3s-invs fut-back-take(TI)-
                                                                theme-3s-PRO
"If you don't give it to me, my father will take it back."

2. Temporal ("when") clauses which refer to the future; most make use of the inchoative prefix a' in the subordinate clause, and the time linker it in the main clause:

(o) Áó'tooyiniki áakitsoyo'pa.
   a'-o'too-yiniki[143] yáak-it-Ioyi-o'pa
   inchoat-arrive(AI)-1s/2s(subj) fut-then-eat(AI)-21
"When you/I arrive, (then) we'll eat."

(p) Ai'sóótaasi, áakitsipiimmiaawa.
   a'-sootaa-si[144] yáak-it-IpiiM:-yi-aawa
   inchoat-rain(II)-in.s(subj) fut-then-enter-3p-PRO
"When it rains, they will go in."

---

[142] New abbreviations here include 'subj' for 'Subjunctive'.

[143] Two glottal stops together (as a result of Glottal Metathesis) are reduced to one. See Appendix B., where this is captured by Glottal Reduction.

[144] s-Connection, which would insert an i before the s of the suffix si, does not apply. Evidently this insertion is blocked before suffixes; see the revised version of s-Connection b in Appendix B.

Iterative temporal antecedent clauses make use of preverb ihkan~kan 'all', and if the main clause verb describes a process, it has the durative prefix:

(q) Kanáísootaasi, itáípiimma.
    kan-á-isootaa-si it-á-IpiiM:-wa
    all-dur-rain(II)-3s(subj) then-dur-enter-3s
    "Whenever it rains, he goes in."

C. THE IMPERATIVE PARADIGMS

These are verb forms used to tell someone to do something. The force of such commands can be softened by use of preverbs such as noohk-, kipp-, and stam-, all of which are difficult to assign a gloss to. In their use with imperatives, however, these preverbs are functional equivalents to English please.

Because the subject of all imperative forms is second person, there are singular and plural forms in each paradigm. The AI and TI forms end in -t if the subject is singular (2s) or in -k if the subject is plural (2p). There are no person prefixes in any imperative paradigm. Here are AI and TI examples:

(r) Ooyít!   Ooyík!   "Eat!"
    ooyi-t   ooyi-k
    eat(AI)-2s(imp)   eat(AI)-2p(imp)

(s) Stámssohksi'poyit!   "Go on, speak loudly!"
    stam-sohk-I'poyi-t
    just-loud-speak(AI)-2s

(t) Noohkohpómmatoot!   Noohkohpómmatook!   "Please buy it!"
    noohk-ohpommatoo-t noohk-ohpommatoo-k
    please-buy(TI)-2s   please-buy(TI)-2p

The TA imperative paradigm has more forms, for it must show agreement with person of the object. As in the other TA paradigms, if the object is first person plural, number of the second person subject cannot be shown (w). Number of a third person object is not reflected (unless an attached pronoun is present, of course). The suffixes used with a third person object lengthen a preceding short vowel (v).

(u) Noohkohkókkit!   Noohkohkókkik!   "Please give it to me!"
    noohk-ohkot-k-i-t   noohk-ohkot-k-i-k
    please-give(TA)-inv-1-2s please-give(TA)-inv-1-2p

(v) Ma'tóós!   Ma'tóók!   "Take it!"
　　ma'to-:s   ma'to-:k
　　take(TA)-2s:3   take(TA)-2p:3

(w) Kippsspómmookinnaaan!   "Please help us!"
　　kipp-sspommo-ok-innaan
　　please-help(TA)-inv-1p

D. THE UNREAL PARADIGMS

The unreal paradigms, used in counterfactual and hypothetical subordinate clauses, and often in the accompanying main clause as well, are essentially the same as the independent paradigms with the addition of markers. These markers follow the corresponding independent form in its entirety, save for 3, 4, and ip suffixes. The markers are -opi, -htopi, -ohtopi, or -wahtopi, depending upon position in the paradigm.[145] Here are some examples:

(x) Nitsítssáyoyihtopi, nitáaksoyi ánnohka.
　　nit-it-say-Ioyi-htopi　nit-áak-Ioyi annohka
　　1-then-neg-eat-unreal　1-fut-eat　now
　　"If I hadn't eaten then, I'd eat now."

(y) Kátá'yo'kaawahtopiyaawa, áaksstaayaawa mááhksoyssaawa.
　　kátá'-yo'kaa-wahtopi-yi-aawa yáak-sstaa-yi-aawa m-ááhk-Ioyi-hsi-aawa
　　neg-sleep-unreal-3p-PRO　fut-want-3p-PRO　3-might-eat-conj-PRO
　　"If they weren't asleep, they'd want to eat."

(z) Nikkámináanatao'topi.　"How I should like to own him!"[146]
　　n-ikkam-inaanat-a-o'topi
　　1-if-own(TA)-dir-unreal

---

[145]I have found differences among speakers, even from the same reserve, in the shape of these forms.

[146]From Uhlenbeck (1938.171).

CHAPTER TWENTY

Nominalizations

There are at least five ways of forming noun stems from verb stems. These will be presented here as: 1. Reclassification; 2. Abstract nominalization; 3. Instrument nominalization; 4. Conjunctive nominalization; 5. Transitive theme nominalization. Then in section 6 we will illustrate their use in complete sentences, showing that most are the functional equivalent of English relative clauses.

1. RECLASSIFICATION

An intransitive verb stem may be used as a noun stem which references the subject of the underlying verb. So for example the AI stem áyo'kaa 'sleep' can serve as a noun stem meaning 'one who sleeps'. Such stems may be complex; in fact, all except stative stems apparently have a tense or aspect prefix - this particular stem has the durative prefix á - and may have any number of other morphemes. Here is a noun utilizing the just-mentioned durative stem for 'sleep':

omiksi áyo'kaiksi   "those sleeping ones"
om-iksi á-Io'kaa-iksi
that-3p dur-sleep-3p

As evidence that we are in fact dealing with a noun, observe that áyo'kaiksi has the plural inflectional suffix iksi which, as we have seen in chapter 2, is used for animate gender nouns.

Here are further examples of reclassification; the first two contain the simplex stem for 'sleep' as in the previous example, but also include additional prefixes in the stem. (Note: Because -wa '3s' is used on both nouns and verbs, singulars of these nominals are often homophonous with a verb form.)

anniksi áakso'kaiksi   "those who will sleep"
ann-iksi áak-Io'kaa-iksi
that-3p fut-sleep-3p

oma áíssáakso'kaawa   "that one who is trying to sleep"
om-wa á-ssáak-Io'kaa-wa
that-3s dur-try-sleep-3s

káta'yáípasskaawa   "non-dancer"
káta'-á-ipasskaa-wa
neg-dur-dance-3s

áókstakiwa   "reader"
á-okstaki-wa
dur-read-3s

Note that in the following example the logical object of the underlying verb is included:

omiksi ííkaayaokstakiiksi sináákia'tsii   "those who have read books"
om-iksi ííkaa-ya-okstaki-iksi sináákia'tsiS-i
that-3p past:perf-dur(?)-read-3p book-nonpartic

anna áóttakiwa   "the bartender"
ann-wa á-ottaki-wa
that-3s dur-serve^drink-3s

anni iyó'kaayi   "the one$_{4s}$ who slept"
ann-yi i-Io'kaa-yi
that-4s past-sleep-4s

2. ABSTRACT NOMINALIZATION

Noun stems are formed from intransitive verbs by addition of -n ~ -hsiN (glossed as 'nom' in the examples to follow); the first allomorph is used with stems ending in -aa, and the second allomorph with other verbs. Such noun stems either refer abstractly to the state or process described by the underlying verb, or in the case of processes which generally result in a product, to the product of that process. For example, when such a noun is formed from the AI verb stem okstaki 'read', the resultant noun stem okstakssiN means 'reading'. If the same suffix is added to sinaaki 'make an image/ write/ draw', the resultant noun will mean either 'writing/drawing' (the processes) or 'written document/ picture' (the products).

Here are examples of nouns formed from aa-final verb stems:

o'kááni "sleep (n.)"
o'kaa-n-yi
sleep-nom-in.s

passkááni "dance (n.)/dancing"
passkaa-n-yi
dance-nom-in.s

sootááni "rain (n.)"
sootaa-n-yi
rain-nom-in.s

isamáá'pawaawahkaanistsi "long (in time) walks"
isamo-a'p-a-wa:wahkaa-n-istsi
long^time-PREF-dur-walk-nom-ip

Examples with other verb stems; note that the third and fourth examples differ only in gender, showing that not all abstract nominals are of inanimate gender:

piókska'ssini 'a long run'
pi-okska'si-hsiN-yi[147]
far-run-nom-in.s

ikkamókstakssini 'fast reading'
ikkam-okstaki-hsiN-yi
fast-read/count(AI)-nom-in.s

sináákssiiksi 'photos/pictures'
sinaaki-hsiN-iksi
make^image(AI)-nom-3p

sináákssiistsi 'writings'
sinaaki-hsiN-istsi
make^image-nom-ip

The subject of the underlying verb may be indicated as a possessor:

nitsskíítaanistsi 'my baked goods'
nit-ihkiitaa-n-istsi
1-bake(AI)-nom-ip

---

[147]This example illustrates that if **ih** is in a position where both Presibilation and Postsibilation are applicable, neither applies and we get only a long **ss**. This is accounted for in Appendix B as **ih-Loss**.

nitsí'nikkssinnaana 'our₁ₚ kill'
nit-i'nikk-ihsiN-nnaan-wa
1-kill(AI)-nom-1p-3s

nóko'sa otsíkkamokska'ssini 'my child's fast running'
n-oko's-wa ot-ikkam-okska'si-hsiN-yi
1-offspring-3s 3-fast-run-nom-in.s

kitáakopissinnoonistsi 'the places we₂₁ will stay'
kit-yáak-opii-hsiN-nnoon-istsi
2-fut-stay-nom-21-ip

kitsipásskaaninnooni 'our₂₁ dancing'
kit-ipasskaa-n-innoon-yi
2-dance-nom-21-in.s

3. ASSOCIATED INSTRUMENT NOMINALIZATION

Nouns which name instruments commonly associated with processes described by specific verbs are readily formed from those verbs. The most productive way of doing this will be illustrated in the section 4.3. The current section presents an apparently old and less productive way of forming such nouns: addition of the suffix <u>a'tsiS</u> to AI stems, as seen in the following examples:

sináákia'tsisi 'book'
sinááki-a'tsiS-yi
make^image-instr-in.s

isttókimaa'tsiistsi 'drums'
isttokimaa-a'tsiS-istsi
drum(AI)-instr-ip

sisóya'tsiiksi 'scissors'
sisoyi-a'tsiS-iksi
cut^in^strips-instr-3p

kaahtsá'tsiistsi 'playing cards'
kaahtsi-a'tsiS-istsi
gamble-instr-ip

oohkóyimaa'tsisa 'lid'
yoohkoyimaa-a'tsiS-wa
cover(AI)-instr-3s

Possessive affixes with such nouns indicate possession or ownership, not the subject of the underlying verb:

    nitokáa'tsisi   'my lariat'
    nit-okaa-a'tsiS-yi
    1-snare(AI)-instr-in.s

    kitsísttókimaa'tsinnooni   'our$_{21}$ drum'
    kit-isttokimaa-a'tsiS-innoon-yi
    2-drum(AI)-instr-21-in.s

4. CONJUNCTIVE NOMINALS

Nominal expressions are formed from both transitive and intransitive verbs by addition of affixes nearly identical to those of the Conjunctive paradigms (see chapter 19 and Appendix A); they differ from corresponding Conjunctive verb affixes in two ways:

1. Where the latter have -hs or -'s, the nominals have -hp (-'p for the 21 forms).[148]

2. They lack the yi suffix which marks all Conjunctive verb forms.

The affixes indicate the person and number of the underlying subject, and, in the case of transitive verbs, of the underlying primary object as well. It is probably more realistic to speak of this phenomenon as **clause nominalization**, for not only do the verbs agree with subject and object, but all other elements which normally accompany verbs in clauses may be present with Conjunctive Nominals. That we are dealing with nominalization here is evident, however, in that the verbs of such clauses occur with nominal suffixes after the Conjunctive affixes, as will be seen in examples below. Note that while most such nominals are classified as inanimate in grammatical gender, many formed from verbs containing the 'instrument/means' prefix (see below) are of animate grammatical gender.

The semantic reference (meaning) of Conjunctive Nominals is determined by makeup of the stem and the syntactic class of the underlying verb. If the verb stem contains a linker (see section 4 of chapter 16), the nominal refers to the linked argument (sections 4.1-4.4). The following examples are grouped according to the linker involved.

---

[148]To utilize the TA Conjunctive Verb chart in Appendix A to form Conjunctive nominals, one must "undo" the effects of Presibilation; *i.e.* certain ss clusters must be recognized as coming from underlying ihs.

4.1 Locational Nominals

These utilize it- ~ iit- 'there':

otsítaniihpi ot-it-wa:nii-hp-yi 3-there-say-nom-in.s	'where he said (something)'
otsítohkitáópiihpi ot-it-ohkit-á-opii-hp-yi 3-there-upon-dur-sit-nom-in.s	'what he's sitting on'
iitáóoyo'pi iit-á-ooyi-o'p-yi there-dur-eat-21:nom-in.s	'where one eats/ restaurant'
iitáísóooyo'pi iit-á-iso-ooyi-o'p-yi there-dur-on-eat-21:nom-in.s	'table (what one eats upon)'
iitáíssiiststakio'pi iit-á-ssiiststaki-o'p-yi there-dur-wash-21:nom-in.s	'where one washes clothes/ laundry'
iitáíssáakio'pi iit-á-ssáaki-o'p-yi there-dur-wipe-21:nom-in.s	'where one washes dishes/ sink'
kitsítáóoyihpoaawayi kit-it-á-ooyi-hp-oaawa-yi 2-there-dur-eat(AI)-nom-2p-in.s	'where you$_{2p}$ eat/ your restaurant'

The preceding examples all involve intransitive verb stems. The following are transitive:

omistsi kitsítsinoohpistsi om-istsi kit-it-ino-o-hp-istsi that-ip 2-there-see(TA)-1:2-nom-ip	'the places I saw you'
nitsítohkoonihpi nit-it-ohkooni-hp-yi 1-there-find(TI)-nom-in.s	'where I found it'

4.2 Temporal Nominals

These utilize a linker it- ~ iit- 'when' which is homophonous with the location linker:

    otsíto'toohpiaawa   'when they arrived'
    ot-it-o'too-hp-yi-aawa
    3-when-arrive-nom-3p-PRO

    otsítaissikópiihpi   'when he rests'
    ot-it-a-ssikópii-hp-yi
    3-when-dur-rest-nom-in.s

    iitáóhkohtao'pi   'November/ when one gathers firewood'
    iit-á-ohkohtaa-o'p-yi
    when-dur-get^wood-21:nom-in.s

4.3 Instrumental Nominals

These involve the 'instrument/means' prefix omoht- ~ iiht- ~ oht-.
Verb stems containing this linker are used extensively to construct vocabulary for items newly introduced to the culture:

    iihtáóoyo'pa   'fork/ what one eats with'
    iiht-á-ooyi-o'p-wa
    instr-dur-eat-21:nom-3s

    iihtáí'poyo'pa   'telephone/ what one speaks with'
    iiht-á-I'poyi-o'p-wa
    instr-dur-speak-21:nom-3s

    iihtáóhpommao'pa   'money/ what one buys with'
    iiht-á-ohpommaa-o'p-wa
    instr-dur-buy-21:nom-3s

    iihtáípissapio'pa   'telescope/ what one sees afar with'
    iiht-á-ipi-ssapi-o'p-wa
    instr-dur-far-look-21:nom-3s

Because such nominals can become conventional names for items, *i.e.* a kind of idiom, it is not too surprising that a given construction can refer to more than one entity, and with these two meanings, be assigned to two gender classes. For example, when the following construction serves as the idiom for 'dish cloth', it is of animate gender. However, when it has its literal meaning it is assigned to the inanimate gender class.

Nominalizations

    iihtáíssáakio'pa   'dish cloth' (anim)
    iihtáíssáakio'pi   'what one wipes with' (inan)

Instrumental Conjunctive nominals may have other than '21/unspecified' as the underlying subject:[149]

   nómohtáóoyihpa   'what I eat with/ my fork'
   n-omoht-á-ooyi-hp-wa
   1-instr-dur-eat-nom-3s

   nomohtsíniihpi   'what I saw it with'
   n-omoht-Inii-hp-yi
   1-instr-see(TI)-nom-in.s

   ómohtoki'takihpi   'the cause of his anger'
   w-omoht-ok-i'taki-hp-yi
   3-means-bad-feel-nom-in.s

   komohtáí'poyihpa   'your telephone'
   k-omoht-a-I'poyi-hp-wa
   2-instr-dur-speak-nom-3s

4.4 Other Linker Nominals

   otsítapoohpistsi   'places he went'
   ot-itap-oo-hp-istsi
   3-toward-go-nom-ip

   otohpióyihpi napayíni   'what he ate the bread with'
   ot-ohp-Ioyi-hp-yi napayín-yi
   3-assoc-eat-nom-in.s bread-in.s

   nítohtahtsówaokska'sspa   'the one in place of whom I ran'
   nit-ohtahtsiwa-okska'si-hp-wa
   1-in^place^of-run-nom-3s

---

[149]Observe that although, as stated above, many conjunctive nominals are idioms, it is the construction *pattern* with certain verbs that is an idiom, and not individual lexical items; for if we were dealing here with individual lexical items as idioms, we would expect that the means of indicating possession of such items would follow the patterns seen in chapter 14, rather than what follows.

4.5 Manner Nominals

If the verb stem contains the abstract manner prefix <u>niit-</u> ~ <u>aanist-</u> (see section D.1 of chapter 16), the nominal refers to the manner of the predication, as illustrated in the following examples:

    maanistániihpi   'the way he said (something)'
    m-aanist-wa:nii-hp-yi
    3-how-say(AI)-nom-is

    kaanistáóoyihpi   'the way you eat'
    k-aanist-á-ooyi-hp-yi
    2-how-dur-eat-nom-in.s

    naanistáótsspi   'the way I swim'
    n-aanist-á-otsi-hp-yi
    1-how-dur-swim-nom-in.s

    niitáótso'pi   'the way one swims'
    niit-á-otsi-o'p-yi
    how-dur-swim-21:nom-in.s

    maanistáípasskaahpoaawayi   'the way they dance'
    m-aanist-á-Ipasskaa-hp-oaawa-yi
    3-how-dur-dance-nom-3p-in.s

    naanistákomimmihpi   'the way he/she loves me'
    n-aanist-akomimm-yi-hp-yi
    1-how-love(TA)-inv:3-nom-in.s

    omi kaanistákomimmokihpi   'the way you love me'
    om-yi k-aanist-akomimm-oki-hp-yi
    that-in.s 2-how-love-inv:1-nom-in.s

4.6 Other Conjunctive Nominals

If the stem does not contain a linker or the abstract manner prefix, the reference of the nominal depends upon the syntactic class of the verb stem.

4.6.1 If the verb stem is paratransitive[150] the resultant nominal refers to the

---

[150]Paratransitive verbs are AI verbs which may occur with non-particular or unspecified objects; see section C. of chapter 7.

Nominalizations

(secondary) object of the underlying verb:[151]

iiyó'pi   'what we$_{21}$ ate'
iiyi-o'p-yi
past:eat-21:nom-in.s

otáániihpoaawaistsi   'things they said'
ot-wa:nii-hp-oaawa-istsi
3-say(AI)-nom-3p-ip

4.6.2 In the case of other intransitive verbs (what might be called "true" intransitives) the resultant nominal refers to the "fact that" the predication takes (or has taken) place:

ánnohka otsó'kaahpi, ...   'now that he's asleep, ...'
annohka ot-Io'kaa-hp-yi
   now   3-sleep-nom-in.s

ánnohka áí'sawayo'kao'pi, ...   'now that we$_{21}$ are not sleeping, ...'
annohka á'-saw-a-Io'kaa-o'p-yi
   now inchoat-neg-dur-sleep-21:nom-in.s

nitsó'kaahpi   '... that I slept'
nit-Io'kaa-hp-yi
1-sleep-nom-in.s

iikská'so'pi   '... that we$_{21}$ ran'
iikska'si-o'p-yi
past:run-21:nom-in.s

nitókska'sspi   '... that I ran'
nit-okska'si-hp-yi
1-run-nom-in.s

4.6.3 Conjunctive Nominals of TI verbs without a linker or the abstract manner prefix refer to the object of the underlying verb:

kitáóowatoohpistsi   'the things you eat'
kit-á-oowatoo-hp-istsi
2-dur-eat(TI)-nom-ip

---

[151] Evidently, such conjunctive nominals are not possible with paratransitive stems ending in aa-; such stems take suffix -n (the nominalizer seen in section 2 above?) instead of hp. For example, one speaker rejected *otsskíítaahpoaawaistsi 'the goods they baked' and preferred otsskíítaanoaawaistsi.

otáánistoohpoaawaistsi 'the things they said'
ot-wáánistoo-hp-oaawa-istsi
3-say(TI)-nom-3p-ip

4.6.4 Conjunctive Nominals of paraditransitive[152] verbs without a linker or the abstract manner prefix refer to the secondary object of the underlying verb:

otsíísoahpiáyi 'what he fed him'
ot-yiiso-a-hp-yi-áyi
3-feed-dir-nom-in.s-PRO

nitáakanistahpi 'what I will tell him'
nit-áak-wa:nIt-a-hp-yi
1-fut-say(TA)-dir-nom-in.s

kitánikkihpoaayi 'what you$_{2p}$ told me'
kit-wa:nIt-ki-hp-oaa-yi
2-say(TA)-inv:1-2p-in.s

iihkótahpi 'what was given to him'
iihkot-a:-hp-yi
past:give(TA)-dir-nom-in.s

omiksi nítohpommááttsaahpiksi nohkówa
om-iksi nit-ohpommaa-áttsi-a:-hp-iksi n-ohkó-wa
that-3p 1-buy(AI)-cause(TA)-dir-nom-3p 1-son-3s
'those which I made my son buy'

otohpómmoahpiáyi 'what he bought for her'
ot-ohpomm-o-a:-hp-yi-áyi
3-buy-ben(TA)-dir-nom-in.s-PRO

4.6.5 For monotransitive TA verbs (*i.e.* those which do not take secondary objects) the Conjunctive Nominal refers to the "fact that" the predication takes (or has taken) place:

kitsikákomimmokihpi 'that you love me'
kit-ikakomimm-oki-hp-yi
2-love(TA)-inv:1-nom-in.s

---

[152]See supplemental material of section C of chapter 7.

5. TRANSITIVE THEME NOMINALIZATION

This section deals with nominals formed from transitive verb stems plus a theme suffix.

5.1 TI Theme Nominals

TI stem + m = noun refering to **subject** of the underlying verb:

omiksi   iihpómmatoomiksi   anni   í'ksisakoyi
om-iksi   iihpommatoo-m-iksi   ann-yi i'ksisako-yi
that-3p   past:buy(TI)-theme-3p   that-in.s meat-in.s
'those who bought that meat'

anna   ákaisínaima   amoyi
ann-wa ákaa-sinai-m-wa   amo-yi
that-3s perf-draw(TI)-theme-3s this-in.s
'the one who drew this'

For this construction, the subject of the underlying verb can only be third person, and the noun is inflected for number only.

5.2 TA Direct Theme Nominals

TA stem + a: = noun referring to the **primary object** of the underlying verb.
    ("the one who the subject VERBs")

This construction is possible only for subject and object combinations which would call for the direct theme suffix (see chapter 10). The resultant noun is inflected to agree with the subject of the underlying verb. The agreement affixes here and in 5.3 are essentially those from the possessive paradigm (see chapter 14), except that "agreement" with 21 is null; *i.e.* the absence of affixes indicates 21. (Note: Here again, because -wa '3s' is used on both nouns and verbs, singulars are often homophonous with a verb form, as indicated in parentheses.) Here are several such nominals, all but the last of which contain TA stem Ino 'see':

nitsíínoannaana	'the one we$_{1p}$ saw' (= 'We$_{1p}$ saw him.')
nitsíínoannaaniksi	'the ones we$_{1p}$ saw'
iinoáwa	'the one we$_{21}$ saw' (= We$_{21}$ saw him.')
iinoáíksi	'the ones we$_{21}$ saw'
otsíínoayi	'the one$_{4s}$ he$_{3s}$ saw'
otohpokóomaiksi	'the ones$_{4p}$ he$_{3s}$ accompanied'

TA stem + yii = noun referring to the **subject** of the underlying verb.[153]
   ("the one who VERBs")

For this construction, the subject of the underlying verb can only be third person, and the underlying object need not be specified. The noun is inflected only for number.[154]

   anniksi i'nitsííksi   'the killers (of someone/something)'
   anniksi i'nitsííksi kitómitaama 'the killers of your dog'
   omiksi iihpokóomiiksi   'those companions (of someone)'
   amo issámmiiwa   'this one who looked at (someone)'

5.3 TA Inverse Theme Nominals

TA stem + Ok = noun referring to **subject** of the underlying verb
   ("the one who VERBs the object")

This construction is possible only for subject and object combinations which would call for the inverse theme suffix (see chapter 11). The resultant noun is inflected to agree with the object of the underlying verb. (Note: Here again, because -wa '3s' is used on both nouns and verbs, singulars are often homophonous with a verb form, as indicated in parentheses below.) Here are several such nominals:

   nitsíínooka   'the one who saw me' (= 'He saw me.')
   nitsíínookiksi   'the ones who saw me'
   nitsíínookinnaana   'the one who saw us$_{1p}$' (= 'He saw us.')
   iinóókiwa   'the one who saw us$_{21}$' (= 'He saw us.')
   otsíínookiksi   'the ones$_{4p}$ who saw him$_{3s}$'
   otsíínookoaawayi   'the one$_{4s}$ who saw them$_{3p}$'
   otsí'nikkiksi   'the ones$_{4s}$ who killed him$_{3s}$'
   otohpokóomokoaawaiksi   'the ones$_{4p}$ who accompanied them$_{3p}$'

---

[153] I have found only a few examples of this construction, and am successful only about one third of the time in attempting to create additional acceptable examples. Further research is needed to determine the subclass of TA verbs which can serve as the base for this construction.

The fact that this type of nominal references underlying **subjects** suggests that the suffix -yii detransitivizes TA verb stems; for if they are intransitive, then such nominalizations would be expected to reference subjects; see section 1.

[154] An apparent example of such a noun with a possessive prefix is: omiksi otohpokóomiiksi 'his companions'; however, this form apparently arose as a mispronunciation of otohpokóomaiksi 'his companions (the ones he accompanied)', seen just above, rather than being a possessed form of the third example below.

6. RELATIVE CLAUSES

Clauses which modify a noun are relatively rare in Blackfoot. It is perhaps a typological characteristic of the language that "free relatives" are used to the near exclusion of relative clauses which modify a noun.[155] In any case, relative clauses utilize most of the nominals presented in the preceding sections of this chapter. (The type of nominalization will be indicated by reference, in square brackets at the end of the noun stem gloss, to a section number of the current chapter.) We begin with a few of the somewhat rare examples of relative clauses which modify a noun. In most such cases, the relative clause follows the noun, though if the relative clause is a single word, it may occur before the noun, as in the third example:

Oma nínaawa áyo'kaawa nóoma.
om-wa ninaa-wa áyo'kaawa n-oom-wa
that-3s man-3s dur-sleep[1.]-3s 1-husb-3s
"That man who is sleeping is my husband."

Omiksi aakííkoaiksi áínihkiiksi áyaakahkayiyaawa.
om-iksi aakííkoaN-iksi á-Inihki-iksi áyaak-wa:hkayi-yi-aawa
that-3p girl-3p dur-sing[1.]-3p fut-go^home-3p-PRO
"Those girls who are singing are on their way home."

Nítssksinoayi anniksi ikkááyiiksi saahkómaapiiksi.
nit-ssksino-a:-yi ann-iksi ikkaayi-iksi saahkómaapi-iksi
1-know(TA)-dir-3p that-3p run^fast[1.]-3p boy-3p
"I know those boys who are fast runners."

The next two examples are sentences found in Uhlenbeck (1938) and have been reelicited. The suffix glossed 'rel' is what Uhlenbeck calls the "relative" suffix. It is frequently found in relative clause constructions, though on the Head noun and demonstrative as well as on the nominal in the relative clause. (It is not clear whether or not this suffix should be identified with the post-inflectional suffix -hka seen in section E of chapter 13.)

Annistssk anákimaa'tsiistssk nitsinííhpistssk ómahkoyaawa.
ann-istsi-hk anakimaa'tsiS-istsi-hk nit-inii-hp-istsi-hk omahko-yi-aawa
that-ip-rel lamp-ip-rel 1-see(TI)-nom[4.6.3]-ip-rel big(II)-ip-PRO
"Those lamps which I saw are big."

---

[155]Though in most cases the "free" relative clause is accompanied by a demonstrative which could conceivably be considered to be a pronoun modified by the relative clause; see section B of chapter 13 regarding demonstratives as pronouns.

Ki tókskamma omíksska ponokáíksska áyiistapokska'siiksska
ki tokskaM:-wa om-iksi-hka ponoká-iksi-hka á-yiistap-okska'si-iksi-hka
and one(AI)-3s that-4p-rel elk-4p-rel dur-away-run[1.]-4p-rel

   iihpókiiyoowa.
   iihpokiiyoo-wa
   follow(AI)-3s

"And one followed those elk that were running away."

The next example has a relative clause which is "extraposed" to the end of the sentence, away from its demonstrative.

Ámi nitáakita'kaa Isapómahksika otsítsstsiihpi.
am-yi nit-yáak-it-wa'kaa Isapómahksika ot-it-ihtsii-hp-yi
here-in.s 1-fut-there-entrench Crowfoot 3-there-lie-nom[4.4]-in.s
"Here I will entrench, where Crowfoot lies (buried)."

As stated above, examples of relative clauses could be constructed with nearly all of the nominalizations presented in this chapter. Here is a sampling, all in complete sentences, of such clauses without a Head noun.

Omiksi áíkkaayiskatsiiksi ííkssoksistómiyaawa.
om-iksi á-ikkaayiskatsi-iksi iik-sok-Istom-i-yi-aawa
that-3p dur-race[1.]-3p very-good-body-have(AI)-3p-PRO
"Those racers have good bodies."

   Iihtaníkkit omistsi kitáakopissinnoonistsi.
   iiht-wa:nIt-k-i-t om-istsi kit-áak-opii-hsiN-nnoon-istsi
of-say(TA)-inv-1-2s(imper) that-ip 2-fut-stay-nom[2.]-21-ip
"Tell me about the places we will be staying!"

Nimáátssksinoaayi omiksi komohtsíístapáaataiksi.
n-Imaat-ssksino-a:-yi om-iksi k-omoht-yIIstap-oo-at-a:-iksi
1-neg-know(TA)-dir-3p that-3p 2-from-away-go-fin(TA)-dir[5.2]-3p
"I don't know those you went away from."

Omá nohkówa omíksi otáyiskai'tataiksi niitá'poki'takiyaiksi.
om-wa n-ohkó-iksi om-iksi ot-á-yiskai'tat-a:-iksi niita'p-oki'taki-yi-aiksi
that-3s 1-son-3s that-3p 3-dur-throw^at(TA)-dir[5.2]-3p real-angry-3p-PRO
"The ones my son was throwing at were really angry."

Ami otsíínihkatsimakki otsítssonao'sskipoka.
am-yi ot-iinihkatsimat-k-yi ot-it-sonao'sskip-ok-wa
that-4s 3-past:name(TA)-inv[5.3]-4s 3-then-kiss(TA)-inv-3s
"The one who named him then kissed him." [Siksika dialect]

Annahka nitohkíímaanahka máátamíwaatsiksi annahka
ann-wa-hka nit-ohkiimaan-wa máát-wa:mi-waatsi(iksi) ann-wa-hka
that-3s-invs 1-wife-3s neg-be-3s:nonaffirm that-3s-invs

iihpómmatoomaahka annihka i'ksisakoyihka; mísstamiwa.
iihpommatoo-m-wa-hka ann-yi-hka i'ksisako-yi-hka misst-wa:mi-wa
past:buy-theme[5.1]-3s-invs that-in.s-invs meat-in.s-invs have^identity-3s

"My wife is not the one who bought the meat; it was some (unknown) person."

CHAPTER TWENTY-ONE

Questions

For every language there are two broad functional types of questions, often referred to as "yes/no" questions, which ask for confirmation or denial of the truth of a proposition, and "content" questions, which ask for other information. Sections A and B deal with these two types.

A. YES/NO QUESTIONS

These make use of what we will refer to as **non-affirmative endings**, either alone, as in (a) - (g), or with an interrogative prefix as seen in (h) - (p). The interrogative prefixes are the same as two of the negative prefixes seen in section A of chapter 16: káta' ~ Ikáta' and sta'. The non-affirmative endings are described below.

(a) Áóoyo'síwaatsiksi?
    á-ooyo'si-waatsiksi
    dur-cook(AI)-3s:nonaffirm
"Is she cooking?"

(b) Áyo'kááwaiksaawa?
    á-yo'kaa-waiksaawa
    dur-sleep-3p:nonaffirm
"Are they sleeping?"

(c) Kítssksinoáwaatsiksi?
    kit-ssksino-a:-waatsiksi
    2-know(TA)-dir-3s:nonaffirm
"Do you$_{2s}$ know her?"

(d) Kitsikákomimmokihpa?
    kit-Ikakomimm-o:k-i-hpa
    2-love-inv-1-nonaffirm
"Do you$_{2s}$ love me?"

(e) Kitáaksstsisoohpoááwa?
    kit-áak-sstsisoo-hpoaawa
    2-fut-go^to^town-2p
"Are you$_{2p}$ going to town?"

(f) Áaksoyó'pa? "Are we$_{21}$ gonna eat?"
 áak-Ioyi-o'pa
 fut-eat(AI)-21

(g) Áaksowatóó'paistsaawa? "Are we$_{21}$ gonna eat them(inan)?"
 áak-Iowatoo'p-aistsaawa
 fut-eat(TI)-in.s:nonaffirm

(h) Káta'yáyo'kááwaiksaawa? "Are they sleeping?"
 káta'-yá-yo'kaa-waiksaawa
 interrog-dur-sleep-3p:nonaffirm

(i) Kátao'kska'síwaatsiksi? "Did he run?"
 káta'-okska'si-waatsiksi
 interrog-run-3s:nonaffirm

(j) Kikáta'yáaka'po'takihpa? "Will you work?"[156]
 k-Ikáta'-yáak-a'p-o'taki-hpa
 2-interrog-fut-PREF-work-nonaffirm

(k) Kikátai'nóókaiksaawa? "Did they see you?"
 k-Ikáta'-Ino-o:k-waiksaawa
 2-interrog-see(TA)-inv-3p:nonaffirm

(l) Kikátai'ihpiyihpoááwa?[157] "Did you$_{2p}$ dance?"
 k-Ikáta'-ihpiyi-hpoaawa
 2-interrog-dance-2p

(m) Kikáta'yáakohkottsspommóóhpa? "Can I help you?"
 k-Ikáta'-yáak-ohkott-sspommo-o-hpa
 2-interrog-fut-able-help(TA)-1:2-nonaffirm

(n) Kátai'sootááwaatsiksi? "Is it raining?"
 káta'-sootaa-waatsiksi
 interrog-rain(II)-s:nonaffirm

(o) Kitáaksstao'ohkottsspommóóhpa? "Can I help you?"
 kit-áak-sta'-ohkott-sspommo-o-hpa
 2-fut-interrog-able-help(TA)-1:2-nonaffirm

---

[156]The sequences of prefixes n̲ or k̲ plus Ikáta' are usually reduced to níta' and kíta', so (j) - (m) would normally be heard as Kíta'yáaka'po'takihpa?, Kítai'nóókaiksaawa?, Kítai'ihpiyihpoááwa?, and Kíta'yáakohkottsspommóóhpa?, respectively.

[157]See **Vowel Epenthesis** in appendix B regarding the extra vowel i̲ in this verb.

(p) Ááhkssta'yaomanííwaatsiksi?   "Might he be telling the truth?"
aahk-sta'-ya-omanii-waatsiksi
might-interrog-dur-be^true-s:nonaffirm

The non-affirmative endings

1. If the subject or primary object of the verb is third person, then one of the following is used according to the gender and number of that subject or object:

-waatsiksi 'animate or inanimate singular'
   [See (a), (c), (i), (n), (p) above.]
-waistsaawa 'inanimate plural' [see (g) above]
-waiksaawa 'animate plural' [see (b), (h), (k) above]

In addition, the final vowel of the verb stem (theme suffix in TA verbs) is accented. [(a-c), (g-i), (k), (n), (p) above]

2. If neither the subject nor primary object is third person, the following are true:

a) -hpa is added if plural suffixes are not called for, *i.e.* neither the subject nor primary object is 1p, 21, or 2p (as in (d), (j) and (o));

b) the word has an additional accent on the penultimate (next-to-last) syllable, as in (e), (f), (l), (m), and (o) (unless it is a short vowel plus h, in which case that syllable is voiceless and so can not carry accent, as in (d) and (j));

c) the final vowel of the word (a in every case) is voiced (in contrast to the usual situation in which word-final short vowels are voiceless); see (d-f), (j-m), and (o).

Supplemental Material

Based upon their form when the third person subject or primary object nominal follows the verb, the third person non-affirmative endings should be viewed as made up of a suffix plus pronominal enclitic. That is, the same reasoning that led to description of -aawa, -áyi, -aiksi, and -aistsi as pronouns in chapter 9 also leads us to recognize these non-affirmative pronouns:

-atsiksi '3s/in.s'
-aiksaawa '3p/4p'
-aistsaawa 'ip'

When these pronouns are not present in questions, the final vowel of the verb is usually voiced.

Compare the following to examples (a), (b), and (g) above:

(q) Áóoyo'síwa kitána?   "Is your daughter cooking?"

(r) Áyo'kááwa kóko'siksi?   "Are your kids asleep?"
(s) Áaksowatóó'pa omistsi?   "Are we$_{21}$ gonna eat those(inan)?"

Observe that the suffix <u>wa</u> in examples such as (q) - (s) (and also (f) below) cannot be identified with the <u>wa</u> previously glossed as '3s'. This <u>wa</u> evidently should be glossed as '3:nonaffirm'.

B. CONTENT QUESTIONS

These can be viewed as requests to supply a value for a variable in an otherwise complete proposition. For example, asking "Who did you see?" in English is equivalent to saying "You saw someone; tell me the identity of that someone." In this example, <u>someone</u> is the variable for which the speaker wants a value supplied. Similarly, "How do you feel?" asks for the value of a variable describing manner.

The following is a sampling of content questions in Blackfoot, arranged according to the class of variables for which a value is requested. Many of these utilize nominalizations described in the preceding chapter. In particular, (a)-(c), (e), (f), and (h)-(j) utilize a nominalized verb to describe the variable for which referential identity is requested. Verbs in content questions frequently, but not always, carry the non-affirmative endings described above.

1. Participant as subject or object

a. Human

(a) Takáa/Tahkáa áwaasai'níwa?   "Who is crying?"
    takáa/tahkáa á-waasai'ni-wa   (more lit: who (is) the crier?")
        who   dur-cry-3s

(b) Tsikáa áínoyííwa?   "Who$_4$ does he$_{3s}$ see?"
    tsikáa á-Ino-yii-wa   (lit: who (is) the one he sees?)
    who:4 dur-see(TA)-dir-3s

(c) Takáa anníksska i'nitsííksska kitómitaami?
    takáa ann-iksi-hka I'nits-ii-iksi-hka kit-omitaam-yi
      who that-3p-invs kill(TA)-dir-3p-invs 2-dog-4s
    "Who are the killers of your dog?"

b. Non-human animate gender

(d) Tsá anistápssíwaatsiksi?   "What is it?"
    tsá anistapssi-waatsiksi
    what be(AI)-3s:nonaffirm

(e) Tsá anistápssíwa annáhka kitohpómmatawahka?
  tsá anistapssi-wa ann-wa-hka kit-ohpommat-a:-wa-hka
  what be(AI)-3:nonaffirm that-3s-invs 2-buy(TA)-dir-3s-invs
  "What did you buy?" (more lit: "What is it that you bought?")

(f) Tsá anistápssíwa ánniksi áyo'kaiksi?
  tsá anistapssi-wa ann-iksi á-yo'kaa-iksi
  what be(AI)-3:nonaffirm that-3p dur-sleep-3p
  "What are they that are sleeping?"

c. Inanimate gender

(g) Tsá anistápííwaatsiksi?   "What is it?"
  tsa anistapii-waatsiksi
  what be(II)-in.s:nonaffirm

There are two ways to question the identity of an inanimate gender variable. The most common way uses the II verb stem <u>anistapii</u> 'be' seen in the previous example:

(h) Tsá anistápííwa anníhka kitohpómmatoohpihka?
  tsá anistapii-wa ann-yi-hka kit-ohpommatoo-hp-i-hka
  what be(II)-3s that-in.s-invis 2-buy(TI)-nom-in.s-invs
  "What did you buy?" (more lit: "What is it that you bought?")

The other way uses a question word <u>ááhsa</u> 'what?':

(i) Ááhsa anníhka kitohpómmatoohpihka?   "What did you buy?"
  ááhsa ann-yi-hka kit-ohpommatoo-hp-i-hka
  what that-in.s-invs 2-buy(TI)-nom-in.s-invs

2. Participant as possessor

(j) Takáa otápotskinááma kitsí'nitawa?   "Whose cow did you kill?"
  takáa ot-apotskinaam-wa kit-I'nit-a-wa
       who 3-cow-3s   2-kill-dir-3s

Notice that even though 'cow' is marked as possessed by third person in (j), it is not demoted to minor third person as predicted by the rule stated in section D of chapter 2. Evidently this is due to the fact that the identity of the possessor is not established, and could even be the speaker or the addressee.

3. Oblique nominal

If the variable is in an oblique relation, it is described by a verb with non-affirmative ending (rather than a Conjunctive nominal as one might expect in view of the preceding content questions); the appropriate linker[158] will be present in the verb, and the appropriate question word will appear at the beginning of the sentence. In addition to the question words takáa, tsikáa, and ááhsa, as well as tsa plus anistapii or anistapssi seen in the examples of 1. above, there is a particular question word tsimá for locational obliques, and an additional verb stem anistsii for questions about time. Examples follow:

(k) Ááhsa kómohto'tóóhpa? "Why did you come?"
 ááhsa k-omoht-o'too-hpa ("What [is it that] you came for?")
 what 2-means-arrive-nonaffirm

(l) Tsá anistápiiwa(atsiksi) kómohto'tóóhpa?
 tsá anistapii-waatsiksi k-omoht-o'too-hpa
 what be(II)-3s:nonaffirm 2-means-arrive-nonaffirm
 "Why did you come?/ By what means did you come?"

(m) Tsimá komohto'tóóhpa? "Where did you come from?"
 tsimá k-omoht-o'too-hpa
 where 2-from-arrive-nonaffirm

(n) Tsimá kitsítokoyihpa? "Where do you live?"
 tsimá kit-it-okoyi-hpa
 where 2-there-dwell-nonaffirm

(o) Tsimá kitáakitapóóhpa? "Where are you going?"
 tsimá kit-áak-itap-oo-hpa
 where 2-fut-to-go-nonaffirm

(p) Tsá anistsííyi kitsítsoyihpoááwa? "When did you$_{2p}$ eat?"
 tsá anistsii-yi kit-it-Ioyi-hpoaawa
 what be^time-? 2-then-eat(AI)-2p:nonaffirm

Observe that 'when' questions concerning the past, as in (p), use verb suffix -yi (glossed '?' because its origin is unkown to me), while those about the future, as in (q), use a Subjunctive affix.

(q) Tsá anistsíísi kitáaksoyihpoááwa? "When will you$_{2p}$ eat?"
 tsá anistsii-si kit-áak-Ioyi-hpoaawa
 what be^time-3s(subj) 2-fut-eat(AI)-2p:nonaffirm

---

[158]See chapter 16, section 4.

To inquire about the location of a human nominal, <u>anna</u> is used:[159]

(r) Anná kitohkíímaana?   "Where is your wife?"
    ann-wa kit-ohkiimaan-wa
    that-3s 2-wife-3s

(s) Annáatsiksi Tsaani?   "Where's John?"
    ann-waatsiksi Tsaani
    that-3s:nonaffirm John

Though this is apparently a specialized use of the demonstrative <u>ann</u>, it evidently functions as a verb, at least in so far as it may take a non-affirmative ending, as seen in (s); however, it does not agree with the human nominal in number, as (t) shows:

(t) Annáatsiksi kóko'siksi?   "Where are your kids?"
    ann-waatsiksi k-óko's-iksi
    that-3s:nonaffirm 2-offspr-3p

The accompanying nominal may itself have a demonstrative:[160]

(u) Anná annáhka kóomahka?   "Where's your husband?"
    ann-wa ann-wa-hka k-óom-wa-hka
    that-3s that-3s-invs 2-husband-3s-invs

Questions about amounts make use of <u>tsá</u> plus a verb root <u>niitsi</u>.

(v) Tsá niitsówa katsikíístsi?   "How many shoes do you have?"
    tsá niitso-wa k-atsikiN-istsi
    what be^number(II)-in.s 2-shoe-ip

(w) Tsá niitsímma kóta'siksi?   "How many horses do you have?"
    tsá niitsiM:-wa k-ota's-iksi
    what be^number(AI)-in.s 2-mount-3p

(x) Tsá niitsíítapiyiwa kóko'siksi?   "How many kids do you have?"
    tsá niitsiitapiyi-wa k-oko's-iksi
    what be^no.(person)(AI)-in.s 2-offspr-3p

Questions asking about manner utilize <u>tsá</u> plus the manner prefix <u>niit</u>- ~ a:nist-:

---

[159]In such questions, <u>ann</u> is more often than not reduced to <u>n</u>. So, for example, (s) below will normally be heard as <u>Náatsiksi Tsaani</u>?.

[160]In fact, fluent speakers from the Blood Reserve insisted that sentences such as (r) and (s) are incomplete without one.

(y) Tsá niitá'pao'takíwaatsiksi? "How does she work?"/
    tsá niit-a'p-a-o'taki-waatsiksi "What kind of work does she do?"
    what manner-PREF-dur-work-3s:nonaffirm

(z) Tsá kaanistáópííhpa? "How are you?"
    tsá k-a:nist-á-opii-hpa (more lit: "How are you staying?")
    what 2-manner-dur-stay-nonaffirm

"Why" questions can be formed utilizing prefix máak ~ Imaak,[161] in addition to the method seen in (k) and (l) above:

    Máakssawahkayíwaatsiksi? "Why didn't she go home?"
    máak-saw-wa:hkayi-waatsiksi
    why-neg-go^home-3s:nonaffirm

    Kimáakaniihtsiksi kááhkahkayssi?
    k-Imáak-wa:nii-htsiksi k-aahk-wa:hkayi-hsi
    2-why-say(AI)-?[162] 2-might-go^home-conj
    "Why did you say you wanted to go home?"

---

[161] máo'k ~ Imao'k in the Peigan dialect.

[162] The suffix htsiksi is an additional nonaffirmative suffix; -hpa could be used in its place here.

CHAPTER TWENTY-TWO

Complement Clause Types

Chapter 19 discussed verb paradigms of subordinate clauses. In this chapter we take a more functional approach, organizing subordinate clauses according to a system of classification that is more semantically based. As will be seen, this results in classes of complements which have some structural unity as well.

A. EMBEDDED 'QUESTIONS'

1. Yes/No Sub-type

The verb of an embedded yes/no question in Blackfoot has inflectional affixes from the Subjunctive paradigm (chapter 19), and has the dubitive prefix ikkám- (glossed 'if'). There is no surface similarity to actual questions; in fact embedded yes/no questions are identical in form to conditional clauses (see section B.1 of chapter 19).

(a) Nohkówa   nitáánikka   ikkámssistsikooyiniki.
 n-ohko-wa nit-wa:nIt-k-wa ikkám-sistsikoo-yiniki
 1-son-3s 1-say(TA)-inv-3s if-tire-1s(subj)
 "My son asked me if I was tired."

(b) Áánistsisa[163]   ikkámáakaistoosi.
 wa:nIt-is ikkám-áak-waistoo-si
 say-2s:3(imper) if-fut-come-3(subj)
 "Ask him if he will come."

---

[163]The final a of áánistsisa is not part of any morpheme per se, but is optionally(?) added to any word which would otherwise end in a consonant.

Complement Clause Types

Supplemental Material

Example (c) is of special interest because the main verb ('know') is inflected to agree with the subject of the complement; *i.e.*, the complement subject is 'copied' as object of the main verb. This is a common process in Blackfoot syntax, and is not limited to subjects; see Frantz 1978, 1979, and 1980.

(c) Áakssksinoyiiwa   ohkóyi   ikkamá'pao'takisáyi.
    áak-ssksino-yii-wa w-ohko-yi ikkám-a'p-a-o'taki-s-áyi
    fut-know(TA)-dir-3s 3-son-4s if-PREF-dur-work-3/4(subj)-PRO
    "He knows whether (or not) his son is working."

2. Content Sub-type

Examples (d) and (e) illustrate embedded 'questions' dealing with the identity of subject or animate object of the complement verb. In such cases, as opposed to those we will deal with next, we find a demonstrative followed by the kind of nominalization we called Reclassification (d) and Inverse Theme nominalization (e) in Chapter 20. Also, note that the accompanying independent verb is inflected to agree with the person whose identity is at issue (this makes (d) ambiguous; it can also mean 'I know the one who is coming.').

(d) Nítssksinoawa   annáhka   áwáaistóówahka.
    nit-ssksino-a:-wa ann-wa-hka á-wa:istoo-wa-hka
    1-know(TA)-dir-3s that-3s-invs dur-come-3s-invs
    "I know who is coming."

(e) Nitáakohkoissksinoawa   annáhka   nitáwaayákiookahka.
    nit-áak-ohkoissksino-a:-wa ann-wa-hka nit-á-wa:yáki-o:k-wa-hka
    1-fut-find^out-dir-3s that-3s-invs 1-dur-hit(TA)-inv-3s-invs
    "I'll find out who hit me."

(f) and (g) deal with a 'value' or identity that is neither subject nor animate primary object of the complement verb (true, the thing bought could be animate, and it is the logical object of the verb 'buy', but the underlying verb in these examples is morphologically intransitive; *i.e.* it is paratransitive - see chapter 7.) In such cases Conjunctive nominals (chapter 20, section 4) are used in the complement; and again, they are the same type used in relative clauses.

(f) Nítssksiniihpa   anníhka   nohkówa   otohpómmaanihka.
    nit-ssksini-hp-wa ann-yi-hka n-ohk-wa ot-ohpommaa-n-yi-hka
    1-know(TI)-theme-3s that-in.s-invs 1-son-3s 3-buy(AI)-nom-in.s-invs
    "I know what my son bought."

(g) Nítssksinoawa   nohkówa   maanístohpommaahpi.
nit-ssksino-a:-wa n-ohk-wa m-aanist-ohpommaa-hp-yi
1-know(TA)-dir-3s 1-son-3s 3-manner-buy(AI)-nom-in.s
"I know {what my son bought / how he purchased}."

Supplemental Material

(f) and (g) differ in two ways. First, in (g) the subject of the complement is copied as object of the matrix verb, while in (f) there is either no copying, or there is copying of the inanimate gender object; one cannot tell, for such copying would be vacuous; the verb 'know' has no intransitive form and the TI stem is the default stem. Second, the presence of preverbal element aanist- makes (g) a manner nominal (chapter 20, section 4.5), while (f) is the type of nominal decribed in sect 4.6.1 of chapter 20.

In (h) we again find the complement verb in the Conjunctive nominal form, in this case referring to the non-instigative cause for the dancing by virtue of the presence of the linker (glossed 'means') that would be present in the corresponding independent verb; compare nomohtsspííyi nitsi'táámssi 'I danced because I was happy.'

(h) Nítssksiniihpa   komohtsspíyihpi.   "I know why you danced."
nit-ssksini-hp-wa   k-omoht-ihpiyi-hp-yi
1-know(TI)-theme-in.s 2-means-dance-conj-in.s

B. EMBEDDED 'COMMANDS'

As we see in (i), such complements in Blackfoot have verbs inflected with affixes from the Conjunctive paradigm plus a prefix ááhk (glossed 'might') which in some contexts seems to mean 'perhaps' or 'non-factive'. This combination of ááhk and conjunct inflection is also found in purpose clauses (see section A.2 of chapter 19) and, as we shall see in the next section, in embedded 'wishes'.

(i) Nitáánistawa   mááhksoyssi.   "I told him to eat."
nit-wa:nist-a:-wa m-ááhk-Ioyi-hsi
1-say(TA)-dir-3s 3-might-eat(AI)-conj

(j) Nitsíkamanistomoawa mááhka'po'takssi. "I asked for a job for him."
nit-Ikamanist-omo-a:-wa m-ááhk-a'po'taki-hsi
1-ask-ben(TA)-dir-3s 3-might-work-conj

C. EMBEDDED 'WISHES'

(k) Nohkówa íksstaawa nááhkahkayssi.
   n-ohko-wa Iksstaa-wa n-ááhk-wa:hkayi-hsi
   1-son-3s want(AI)-3s 1-might-go^home-conj
   "My son wants me to go home."

(l) Nohkówa nitsíksstakka nááhkahkayssi.
   n-ohko-wa nit-Iksstat-k-wa n-ááhk-wa:hkayi-hsi
   1-son-3s 1-want(TA)-inv-3s 1-might-go^home-conj
   "My son wants me to go home."

(m) Nitáíksimsstaa nitohkíímaana mááhka'pao'takssi.
   nit-á-Iksimsstaa nit-ohkiimaan-wa m-ááhk-a'p-a-o'taki-hsi
   1-dur-think(AI) 1-wife-3s 3-might-PRE-dur-work-conj
   "I'm thinking of (anticipating) my wife working."

(n) Nitáíksimsstatawa nitohkíímaana mááhka'pao'takssi.
   nit-á-Iksimsstat-a:-wa nit-ohkiimaan-wa m-ááhk-a'p-a-o'taki-hsi
   1-dur-think(TA)-dir-3s 1-wife-3s 3-might-PRE-dur-work-conj
   "I'm thinking of (anticipating) my wife working."

Examples (k) and (l) are synonymous, as are (m) and (n); the second of each pair differs only in that the complement subject is 'copied' as matrix object (see Supplementary Material in section A.1.). More important for our purposes here, the complement verb has the non-factive prefix <u>ááhk</u> and inflectional affixes from the Conjunctive paradigm.

(o) and (p) both have Conjunctive nominal endings instead of just Conjunctive endings on the complement verb, suggesting that such complements don't belong with the embedded 'wishes' in our classification. (o) and (p) differ in that in (o) the complement is subject of 'hard', while in (p) 'dried meats' is subject of 'hard'.

(o) Iiksíyikowa ááhkanistsipikksstsiihpi káyiistsi.
   iik-Iyiko-wa ááhk-a:nist-Ipikkssti-hp-yi kayi-istsi
   very-hard(II)-in.s might-manner-chew(TI)-nom-in.s dried^meat-ip
   "It's hard to chew dried meat."

(p) Káyiistsi iiksíyikoyi ááhkanistsipikksstsiihpi.
   kayi-istsi iik-Iyiko-yi ááhk-a:nist-Ipikkssti-hp-yi
   dried^meat-ip very-hard(II)-ip might-manner-chew(TI)-nom-in.s
   "Dried meats are hard to chew."

References

Bloomfield, Leonard. 1946. Algonquian. Harry Hoijer, ed., Linguistic Structures of Native America. Viking Fund Publications in Anthropology 6.85-129.

Fox, Jacinta and D. Frantz. 1979. Blackfoot clitic pronouns. William Cowan, ed., Papers of the Tenth Algonquian Conference, 152-166. Ottawa.

Frantz, D. G. 1971. Toward a Generative Grammar of Blackfoot. Summer Institute of Linguistics P.L.R.F. #34. Norman, Okla.

Frantz, D. G. 1978. Copying from complements in Blackfoot. Eung-Do Cook and Jonathan Kaye, eds., Linguistic Studies of Native Canada, 89-110. University of British Columbia Press. Vancouver.

Frantz, D. G. 1979. Multiple dependency in Blackfoot. Proceedings of the Fifth Annual Meeting of the Berkeley Linguistic Society, 77-80. Berkeley.

Frantz, D. G. 1980. Ascensions to subject in Blackfoot. Proceedings of the Sixth Annual Meeting of the Berkeley Linguistics Society, 293-299. Berkeley.

Frantz, D. G. and Eugene Creighton. 1982. The indefinite possessor prefix in Blackfoot. William Cowan, ed., Papers of the Thirteenth Algonquian Conference, 137-142. Ottawa.

Frantz, D. G. and Norma J. Russell. 1989. Blackfoot Dictionary of Stems, Roots, and Affixes. University of Toronto Press.

Taylor, Allan R. 1967. Initial change in Blackfoot. Contributions to Anthropology: Linguistics I, Bulletin 214 of National Museum of Canada, 147-156. Ottawa.

Taylor, Allan R. 1969. A Grammar of Blackfoot. Unpublished PhD dissertation, University of California, Berkeley.

Taylor, Allan R. 1978. Deictics in Algonkian. Ms. (Paper read at 83rd annual meeting of the American Anthropological Association, Los Angeles.)

Thomson, Gregory. 1978. The origin of Blackfoot geminate stops and nasals. Eung-Do Cook and Jonathan Kaye, eds., Linguistic Studies of Native Canada, 249-254. University of British Columbia Press. Vancouver.

Uhlenbeck, C. C. 1938. A Concise Blackfoot Grammar. North Holland Publishing Co. Amsterdam.

Appendix A: Verb Paradigms

1. INTRANSITIVE VERB PARADIGMS

	number → subject person	singular	plural
Independent	1	nit-	nit-...-hpinnaana
	2	kit-	kit-...-hpoaawa
	21	-----	-o'pa
	3	-wa	-yi
	4	-yini	-yi
Conjunctive	1	nit-...-hsi	nit-...-hsinnaani
	2	kit-...-hsi	kit-...-hsoaayi
	21	-----	-o'si
	3/4	ot-...-hsi	ot-...-hsi
Subjunctive	1	-iniki	-innaaniki
	2	-iniki	-inoaainiki
	21	-----	-o'ki
	3/4	-si	-si
Unreal[164]	1	nit-...-htopi	nit-...-hpinnaanopi
	2	kit-...-htopi	kit-...-hpoaawopi
	21	-----	-o'topi
	3	-wahtopi	-wahtopiyi
	4	-wahtopiyini	-wahtopiyi
Imperative		-t	-k

---

[164]The 3 and 4 forms in Uhlenbeck (1938, pg. 170) lack the <u>aht</u> portion of the suffixes shown here.

2. TRANSITIVE INANIMATE VERB PARADIGMS

subj	Independent	Conjunctive	Subjunctive	Imperative	Unreal[2]
1s	nit..hp	nit..hsi	...mmiiniki		nit..htopi
1p	nit..hpinnaan	nit..hsinnaani	...mmiinainiki		nit..hpinnaan(oht)opi
2s	kit..hp	kit..hsi	...mmiiniki	...t	kit..htopi
2p	kit..hpoaa	kit..hsoaayi	...mmiinoainiki	...k	kit..hpoaaw(oht)opi
21/x	...'p	...hsi	...i'ki		...'pohtopi
3s	...ma	ot...hsi	...isi		...mahtopi
3p/4p	...mi	ot..hsi	...isi		...mahtopiyi
4s	...mini	ot..hsi	...isi		...mahtopiyini

To the first five Independent forms, add -wa if the object is singular, or -yi if the object is plural.

Note: Several of these suffixes differ from those shown in Uhlenbeck 1938, page 170.

Appendix A: Verb Paradigms

3. TRANSITIVE ANIMATE VERB INDEPENDENT PARADIGM

Obj → Subject	1s	1p	2s	2p	21	3s	3p	4s	4p	5
1s			kit- -o:	kit- -o:hpoaawa		nit- -a:wa	nit- -a:yi	nit- -a:yini	nit- -a:yi	
1p			kit- -o:hpinnaan	kit- -o:hpinnaan		nit- -a:nnaana	nit- -a:nnaani	nit- -a:nnaanini	nit- -a:nnaani	
2s	kit- -Oki	-kit -Okihpinnaan				kit- -a:wa	kit- -a:yi	kit- -a:yini	kit- -a:yi	
2p	kit- -Okihpoaawa	kit- -Okihpinnaan				kit- -a:waawa	kit- -a:waayi	kit- -a:waayini	kit- -a:waayi	
21						-a:wa	-a:yi	-a:yini	-a:yi	
x	nit- -Okoo	nit- -Otsspinnaan	kit- -Okoo	kit- -Otsspoaawa	-Otssp	-a:wa	-a:yi	-a:yini	-a:yi	
3s	nit- -Oka	nit- -Okinnaana	kit- -Oka	kit- -Okoaawa	-Okiwa			-yiiwa	-yiiwa	
3p	nit- -Oki	nit- -Okinnaani	kit- -Oki	kit- -Okoaayi	-Okiyi			-yiiyi	-yiiyi	
4s	nit- -Okini	nit- -Okinnaanini	kit- -Okini	kit- -Okoaayini	-Okiyini	ot- -Okoaayi	ot- -Okoaayi			-yiiyini
4p	nit- -Oki	nit- -Okinnaani	kit- -Oki	kit- -Okoaayi	-Okiyi	ot- -Oka	ot- -Okoaayi			-yiiyi
5								ot- -Okini	ot- -Okoaayini	

Note: On this and the following charts, 'x' in the subject column represents 'unspecified'; see sect. D of both chapters 11 and 12 regarding realization of O. See sect. B of chapter 15 regarding variable-length a: and o:; see sect. D of both chapters 10 and 12.

4. TRANSITIVE ANIMATE VERB CONJUNCTIVE PARADIGM

Obj →	1s	1p	2s	2p	21	3s/3p	4s/4p
Subject							
1s			kit- -o:hsi	kit- -o:hsoaayi		nit- -a:hsi	nit- -a:hsi
1p			kit- -o:hsinnaani	kit- -o:hsinnaani		nit- -a:hsinnaani	nit- -a:hsinnaani
2s	kit- -Okssi	-kit -Okssinnaani				kit- -a:hsi	kit- -a:hsi
2p	kit- -Okssoaayi	kit- -Okssinnaani				kit- -a:hsoaayi	kit- -a:hsoaayi
21						-a:hsi	-a:hsi
x	nit- -Okoohsi	nit- -Otsspinnaani	kit- -Okoohsi	kit- -Otssoaayi	-Otssi	-a:hsi	-a:hsi
3s/3p	nit- -yssi	nit- -yssinnaani	kit- -yssi	kit- -yssoaayi	ot- -Okssi		ot- -aahsi
4s/4p						ot- -yssi	

Note: Stem-final t is dropped before TA Conjunctive suffixes which start with <u>yss</u> (all from <u>yihs</u>.

Appendix A: Verb Paradigms

5. TRANSITIVE ANIMATE VERB SUBJUNCTIVE PARADIGM

Obj → / Subject	1s	1p	2s	2p	21	3s	3p	4s/4p
1s			-iniki	-inoainiki		-a:iniki	-a:iniki	
1p			-innaaniki	-inoainiki		-a:nnaaniki	-a:nnaaniki	
2s	-Okiiniki					-a:iniki	-a:iniki	
2p	-Okiinoainiki					-a:inoainiki	-a:inoainiki	
21						-a:hki	-a:hki	
x	-Okoiniki	-Okoinnaaniki	-Okoiniki	-Okoinoainiki	-Otsski	-a:hki	-a:hki	
3s/3p	-Otsiiniki	-Okisi	-Otsiiniki	-Otsiinoainiki	-Okisi	-Otsiiniki	-Otsiinoainiki	-a:si
4s/4p	**

6. TRANSITIVE ANIMATE VERB IMPERATIVE PARADIGM

Obj → / Subject	1s	1p	3
2s	-Okit	-Okinnaan	-(i)s[1]
2p	-Okik	-Okinnaan	-ok

[1] This suffix has the form -is only after a consonant; otherwise it is -s, but requires that the preceding vowel be lengthened if not already long.

Appendix B: Phonological Rules

1. **GEMINATION** $\quad\quad C_1 \rightarrow C_2 / \_+C_2$

   nitánIt + k + wa → nitánIkk + wa (7,15. → nitánikka) "He told me."

2. **s - INSERTION** $\quad\quad \emptyset \rightarrow s / I\_t$

   nitánItawa → nitánIstawa (7. → nitánistawa) "I told him."

3. **s - CONNECTION**   a. $\emptyset \rightarrow s / C+\_s$

   nit + siksipawa → nítssiksipawa "I bit him"
   nit + ssikópii → nítsssikópii 'I rested'

                            b. $\emptyset \rightarrow i / V(')+\_s,$
   where s̲ is not part of a suffix.

   á + sínaakiwa → áisínaakiwa (25. → áísínaakiwa) "he writes"
   nikáá+ ssikópii → nikáá+ issikópii (10,25. → nikáíssikópii) "I have rested"
   káta' + simiwa → káta'+isimiwa (19. → kátai'simiwa?) "Did she drink?"

4. **o - REPLACEMENT**[165]

                            $o \rightarrow a / \_+a,$ where +a̲ is not a suffix

   áakoto + apinniiwa → áakotaapinniiwa "he will go adjust it"

5. **COALESCENCE** $\quad\quad wi(:) \rightarrow o$

   w + ínni → ónni "his father"
   w + iihsíssi → ohsíssi "her younger sibling"

6. **BREAKING** $\quad\quad k \rightarrow ks / \_I$

   áak + Ipiima → áaksIpiima (7. → áaksipiima) "she will enter"

7. **NEUTRALIZATION** $\quad\quad I \rightarrow i$

   áaksIpiima → áaksipiima "she will enter"

---

[165] For many speakers (perhaps a large percentage), the o̲ of this rule is deleted rather than being replaced by a̲. The rule for such speakers is as follows: $o \rightarrow \emptyset / \_+a$.

Appendix B: Phonological Rules

8. DESYLLABIFICATION $\{ i \rightarrow y, o \rightarrow w \} / V+\_V$
constraint: the i and o are unaccented

kitsí'powata + oaawa → kitsí'powatawaawa "you$_{2p}$ spoke harshly of, or to, him"
(á + Io'kaa + wa 7. →) áio'kaawa → áyo'kaawa "he sleeps"

9. SEMIVOWEL DROP $G \rightarrow \emptyset / \#\_$

yaatóót → aatóót "howl!"
waaníít → aaníít "say (something)!"
w + óko'si → óko'si "his child"

10. VOWEL SHORTENING $V_i: \rightarrow V_i / \_+V$

áyo'kaa + o'pa → áyo'kao'pa "we$_{21}$ sleep"
imitáá + iksi → imitáiksi (25. → imitáíksi) "dogs"

11. i - LOSS[166] $i \rightarrow \emptyset / Vy\_\{a,o\}$

áyo'kaa + yi + aawa → áyo'kaayaawa "they sleep"
áíhpiyi + o'pa → áíhpiyo'pa "we$_{21}$ dance."

12. i - ABSORPTION $i \rightarrow \emptyset / s\_\{a,o\}$

áókska'si + o'pa → áókska'so'pa "we$_{21}$ run"
(nit + Ioyi 7,17. →) nitsioyi → nítsoyi "I ate"

13. ih-LOSS $ih \rightarrow \emptyset / s\_s$

otokska'si + hsi → otóokska'ssi "that he ran"

14. PRESIBILATION[167] ihs → ss
iihs → iss

otá'po'taki + hsi → otá'po'takssi "that he worked"
pii + hsini → pissini "entering"

---

[166]For some speakers, i-Loss is accompanied by lengthening of the preceding V if that V is also an i; e.g., áókstaki+yi+aawa → áókstakiiyaawa.

[167]For a large sub-dialect on the Blood reserve, this process is generalized to the following: ih → s, and iih → is. At the other extreme, there are also a few speakers for whom presibilation is not applicable at all in careful speech.

15. **SEMIVOWEL LOSS**   G → ∅/ C_ , where C ≠ '

áak + yaatoowa → áakaatoowa   "she will howl"
nit+waanii → nitáánii   "I said (something)"
(*cf.* kikáta' + waaniihpa → kikáta'waaniihpa   "Are you saying [something]?")

16. **y - REDUCTION**[168]   iyi → ii / C_y

áíhpiyi + yináyi → áíhpiiyináyi   "he₄ dances"

17. **POSTSIBILATION**   ih → s / s_

aókska'si + hpinnaan → aókska'sspinnaan   "we₁ₚ run"

18. **t - AFFRICATION**   t → ts /_i

nit + it + itsiniki → nitsítsitsiniki   "then I told a story"

19. **GLOTTAL METATHESIS**   'V → V'/ V_C

á' + omai'takiwa → áo'mai'takiwa (25. → áó'mai'takiwa   "**now** he believes"

20. **GLOTTAL LOSS**   ' → ∅ / VV:_C

(káta' + ookaawaatsi 19. →) kátaoo'k... → kátaookaawaatsi
        "Did she sponsor a Sundance?"
[*NB*: V: must be an underlyingly long V, not a variable length V.]

21. **GLOTTAL ASSIMILATION**   Vᵢ' → Vᵢ: / _(s)C: , where C ≠ s

(káta' + ottakiwaatsi 19. →) kátao'tt... → kátaoottakiwaatsi
        "Is he a bartender?"
(á' + isttohkohpiy'ssi 19. →) ái'sttohk... (25. → áíisttohkohpiy'ssi)
        "when he fell down"

22. **GLOTTAL REDUCTION**   ' → ∅ /_'

(á' + o'tooyiniki 19. →) áo''tooyiniki → áo'tooyiniki (25. → áó'tooyiniki)
        "when you arrive"

---

[168]Some speakers maintain the y, at least in careful speech, so it is generally indicated in written Blackfoot materials, including the examples in this book.

Appendix B: Phonological Rules

23. VOWEL EPENTHESIS[169] $\emptyset \rightarrow V_i / V_i\text{'}\_h$

(káta' + ohto'toowa 19. →) kátao'hto'toowa → kátao'ohto'toowa
"Did he arrive from there?"

24. sss - SHORTENING $sss \rightarrow ss / \_C$

(nit + ssksinoawa 3a. →) nitsssksinoawa → nítssksinoawa
'I know him'

25. ACCENT SPREAD $V \rightarrow [+accent] / \underset{[+accent]}{V} + \_$

á+ okska'siwa → áókska'siwa   "he runs"
atsikí + istsi →
atsikíístsi   "shoes"
(kakkóó + iksi 10. →) kakkó+iksi) → kakkóíksi   "pigeons"

INTERACTION CONSTRAINTS

Rules apply for maximal "feeding" and minimal "bleeding" except that 5 bleeds 9, 14, and 15; 12 bleeds 8, and 1 bleeds 2. Rule 8 bleeds 25, but does not bleed nor feed any other rules.

---

[169]In place of this rule, some speakers have the following rule: ' → ∅ / _h. For such speakers, "Did he arrive from there?" would be Kátaohto'toowa.

Index

: in glosses 112

abstract manner prefix 124
accent 3
ACCENT AND LENGTH 65
ACCENT ON DEMONSTRATIVES 65
accent rules 34
Accent Spread 28, 155
ACCOMPANIMENT VERB STEMS 106
acute accent 3
addressee 15, 16, 17, 18, 21, 22, 63
adjuncts 84
ADVERBIAL PREFIXES 91
adverbials 84
AFFIX POSITIONS 56
AGR1 56, 59
AGR2 56, 59
AGR3 56
AGREEMENT 20, 21, 22, 35, 37, 40, 43, 44, 56, 57, 60, 69, 71, 72, 74
agreement affix positions 59
AI 39
allomorphs 78
Allomorphy 78
animate gender 7
Animate Intransitive 39
antecedent 113
ASPECT 30, 96
associative 94
Attached Pronouns 47

ben 104
BENEFACTIVE VERB STEMS 104
bleeding 28, 155
bleeds 28
breaking 31, 32, 35, 152
breaking *I* 31

C = consonant 26

Causative Stems 102
clause nominalization 120
Coalescence 70, 152
Coalescence 2 70, 82
Complement 112
Complex verb stems 84
conditional 110
conj = conjunctive 111
Conjunctive 110
Conjunctive Nominals 93, 120
CONJUNCTIVE PARADIGMS 111
connective I 78
consequent 112, 113
CONSONANT LENGTH 5
CONSONANTS 4
CONTENT QUESTIONS 135
Conventions in interlinear analysis 31
counterfactual 115

Degree 93
demonstrative stems 63
Demonstratives 63
Demonstratives as free pronouns 64
derivational suffix 102
Desyllabification 52, 153
Dictionary 7
diminutives 63
DIPHTHONG 2, 3, 33
Diphthongization 83
dir 55
DIRECT THEME 55, 57, 60
Direct Theme Nominals 127
direct theme suffix 81
directionals 93
Distinct Third Person (DTP) 48
DTP = Distinct Third Person 48
dur 33
DURATIVE ASPECT 32

Embedded clauses 111
Embedded 'questions' 140

enclitic pronouns 47
exclusive we 17
extraposed relative clause 130

falling pitch 3, 90
familiarity 63
feeding 28, 155
feeds 28
final 99
final vowel 134
finals, abstract 99
finals, concrete 99, 102
finals, instrumental 101
free relative 129
fut 31
FUTURE TENSE 31

G 26
G = glide (semivowel) 26
GEMINATION 152
GENDER 7
glide 26, 70
glides 4
GLOTTAL ASSIMILATION 154
GLOTTAL LOSS 154
Glottal Metathesis 85, 154
Glottal Reduction 113, 154
Goal 49

Head 99, 102
Heads 67
hypothetical 115

i - ABSORPTION 153
i - LOSS 153
i-Absorption 57, 70
i-Loss 27, 47, 57
ih-LOSS 153
II 39
imminent future 32
imp 114
Imperative Paradigms 114
in.s = inanimate singular 48
inalienably possessed stems 71
Inanimate Intransitive 39
inanimate gender 7
Inanimate Intransitive affixes 40
INANIMATE LOGICAL
    SUBJECT of TA 61
INANIMATE LOGICAL
    SUBJECT 45
inchoat(ive) 97
inchoative 113
inclusive we 17

inclusive 'our' 69
indefinite possessor 73
independent clause 22
independent pronouns 21, 75
INFLECTIONAL AGREEMENT 40
initial change 36
INITIAL NASAL LOSS 72
initial variation 78
instr 95
Instrument 49, 95
Instrumental Nominals 122
intensifiers 84
INTERACTION OF RULES 28
interrog 133
interrogative prefix 132
intransitive 15, 20, 22, 39, 40, 41, 82
inv 55
INVERSE SUFFIX 57
INVERSE THEME 55, 56, 57, 60, 61
INVERSE THEME NOMINALS 128
invs 66
ip = inanimate plural 47
irrealis 85
irregular variation 78

kin terms 65

linked oblique 112
linker 120, 137
Linkers 94
linking prefix 45, 61
Location 49
Locational Nominals 121

MAJOR THIRD PERSON 11, 12, 13,
    15, 20, 22, 49, 56
Manner 91, 93
manner nominals 124
manner prefix 138
maximal feeding 28
means 95
medial 99
METEOROLOGICAL VERBS 23,
    102
minimal bleeding 28
MINOR THIRD PERSON 11, 12, 13,
    14, 49, 56, 110, 136
modified nouns 10
modifiers 64, 67
modify 64
monotransitive TA verbs 126
MORPHEME 13
MORPHEME-FINAL
    ALLOMORPHY 81

Index

MORPHEME-INITIAL VARIATION 78
movg 66

nasal-initial morphemes 72
nasal-loss alternation 80
neg 84
NEGATION 84
negative 16
negative prefix 84
negatives 84
Neutralization 32, 152
nom 117, 118, 121
nominal 39
Nominalizations 116
non-affirmative endings 132
non-affirmative pronouns 50, 134
non-affirmative suffixes 84
non-factive 111
non-particular 11, 41
non-permanent consonants 9, 81
non-referring 10
non-suppositional cause 112
nonaffirm 132
nonparticular 10
NOUN NUMBER 8
noun stem 7
NOUN SUFFIXES 13
null 26

o - ASSIMILATION 152
o-Replacement 90
o.t. 66
object 15, 40, 41, 43, 44, 45, 47, 49, 51, 52, 55, 56, 59
object, primary 42
object, secondary 41, 42
OBLIGATORILY POSSESSED STEMS 71
oblique 94, 112, 137
obviative 12
OPTIONALLY POSSESSED STEMS 70

paradigm 43
paraditransitive 42
paraditransitive verbs 126
paratransitive 41, 124, 141
particular 10
particular in reference 10
PAST TENSE 35
perf 34
PERFECTIVE ASPECT 34
person 15, 55

person agreement prefixes 37
PERSON MARKERS; see also *person agreement* and *agreement affix* 15
person prefixes 53
person, third 56
phonological rule 25
phonological rules 152
pitch 3
pitch accent 3
please 114
plural 8
pluralize 52, 59
pluralizer 13
pluralizers 52
poss 72
POSSESSIVE AFFIX PARADIGM 74
possessive affixes 69
Possessives 69
POST-INFLECTIONAL SUFFIXES 65
Postsibilation 26, 61, 154
precedence relations 57
PREDICATE ADJECTIVE 22
PREDICATE NOMINATIVE 23
PREF 33
prefix 15
prepositions 94
PRESIBILATION 153
primary object 103, 42, 112, 134
primary referent 71
PRO 47
pronoun 47, 48, 49, 50, 52, 64
pronoun, free 64
pronoun, independent 21
pronouns, independent 75
Pronunciation 18, 32
proximity 63
pseudo-intransitive verbs 41
Purpose clauses 111

quantifiers 84, 87
Questions 132

recipr 108
RECIPROCAL VERB STEMS 107
RECLASSIFICATION of verb stems as noun stems 116
refl 107
REFLEXIVE VERB STEMS 107
rel 129
relatee 71
Relational nouns 72
relational stems 71

relative clauses 116, 129
relative roots 94
rewrite rule 25
root, verb 100
rule interaction 155

s - CONNECTION 152
s - INSERTION 152
s-Connection a 87
s-Connection b 89
second person prefix 35
secondary object 41, 42, 103, 104, 112, 125, 126
semantic classes 23
Semivowel alternation 82, 100
Semivowel Drop 70, 153
Semivowel Loss 26, 28, 47, 55, 154
SEMIVOWELS 4
short form of person agreement prefixes 35, 70
singular 8, 9, 11, 19
source 95
sss - SHORTENING 155
stat 66
stem 7
STEM AGREEMENT 39
stems, complex 99
stems, simplex 99
subcategorized 39, 102
subcategory 39
subj 113
subj = Subjunctive 113
subject 111, 134
Subjunctive 110
Subjunctive Paradigms 112, 113
Subjunctive paradigm 140
Subordinate Clauses 110
sucategorization 40
suffix 15
SUFFIXES 13
Suppositional antecedent 113
SYNTAX 39

t - AFFRICATION 154
t-Affrication 25
TA 40
Temporal clauses 111
Temporal Nominals 122

TENSE 30, 31, 37
theme 44
theme suffix 134
TI 40
TI THEME NOMINALS 127
TI theme suffix 44
toward^spkr 96
transitive 15, 40, 43
Transitive Animate (TA) 40
Transitive Inanimate (TI) 40

Underlying grammatical relations 102
underspecified 83
unlinked nominals 102
unreal 85
Unreal Paradigms 115
unspecified 44, 60, 73
unspecified object 41
unspecified possessor 73
UNSPECIFIED SUBJECT 52

V = vowel 26
VARIABLE-LENGTH VOWELS 80
verb stem 15
VERB STEM TYPES 39
voiceless vowels 18
VOWEL EPENTHESIS 155
VOWEL LENGTH 2
Vowel Shortening 26, 153
VOWELS 1

what 136
what? 135
when? 137
where? 137
who? 135
whose? 136
why? 137, 139
word 7

y - REDUCTION 154
YES/NO QUESTIONS 132
you$_{pl}$ 17

zero 26

^ 67